An Awfully Big Adventure *– Dying to Live*

Some ideas which helped me to live while I died

Chris Braithwaite

Chris Braithwaite 06.05.55 – 19.12.19

Contents

Chris died before completing the end of Chapter 4 and Chapter 5 which is presented here in note form.

Foreword

I find myself in the bizarre, almost embarrassing situation of being alive nearly two years after receiving the diagnosis of terminal cancer. Alongside my husband we have navigated unchartered waters and, much to our surprise, discovered unlooked for riches in terms of improved relationships and quality of life. But we are also changed beyond recognition. What follows is therefore primarily an attempt to make sense of our experiences for ourselves, so that this period of transition allows me to move on and R to remain behind, with as much peaceful acceptance as possible.

Equally, we realise that there are so many taboos surrounding death, that it could be immensely valuable to challenge these in such a way that others can not only bear to consider their own death and that of those closest to them, but also change the way in which they live out their remaining time. After all, the reality is, for those of us receiving the news our life expectation is limited, there remains so very much that science cannot tell us to help us prepare for what lies ahead. This places the majority of us at a very real disadvantage since we in the west have been conditioned to expect that if we study hard or apply ourselves long enough, there is nothing we can't control. The resulting wake-up call however, can be as life changing as Marley's ghost's visit to Scrooge.

We learn many things on this long, sometimes strange journey we see as life, but we mostly find ourselves. Who we really are, what matters most to us. We learn from peaks and valleys what love and relationships really are. We find the courage to push through our anger, tears and fears. In the mystery of all this we have been given all we need to make life work – to find happiness. Not perfect lives, not story book tales, but authentic lives that can make our hearts swell with meaning

Life Lessons- how our mortality can teach us about life and living. Elizabeth Kubler-Ross and David Kessler

The imminence of our death can suddenly make us horribly aware that unless we make major changes, whilst our *Bucket Lists* may just keep getting longer, we will risk learning the real meaning of Life too late to benefit from its lessons. Rather than *'working on our smallness, getting rid of our negativity and finding the best in ourselves and each other … that part that transcends all we have been through and delivers us to all we are capable of doing and being,* our unfinished business will continue to get in the way of us *'not just being alive, but to feeling alive'.*

Instead, I want to suggest that it is possible to celebrate the process of dying in the same way that we celebrate being born. Yes, both may well be painful and messy, but I want to record with passion what it's like to mine its seams, to explore the potential treasures contained in the spiritual insights, that may only become apparent when all the distractions and white noise have been quietened.

So, since I've already discovered that it's too easy to forget hard won insights and working on the premise that *we teach best what we most need to learn'*, the outline I have adopted represents my *Rough Guide to Mortality*. Part SWOT analysis of the Strengths, Weaknesses, Opportunities and Threats that we bring from our current way of living to the prospect of dying; and part Air Traffic Control, implementing safety standards allowing us to invest in advance in the equivalent of flight charts and oxygen masks to make our journey to a good death as smooth as possible.

Chuntering to myself at 4am most mornings however, quickly moved on to checking out with friends to gauge their reactions to the controversial conclusions I was drawing, as a result of having the space to join the dots. Being diagnosed with a life limiting condition then ratcheted everything up still further when I was shocked by how few people shared my belief that this meant simply that I was facing a process of transformation, in much the same way that a caterpillar's life apparently "ends" before it becomes a butterfly. But I've simply known too many people lose the last chunk of their life chasing illusory medical solutions and read enough descriptions of the blissful experiences recounted by those surviving 'Near Death Experiences' (NDE's); not to buy into the *"death is the end"* and/or *"life at all costs"* attitude.

As events unfolded R and I found ourselves forced on a daily basis to come face to face with the taboos surrounding death, not least within the medical profession. This segued into considering another "big" question encountered frequently in my working life, namely the reason behind the amount of debilitating depression experienced by those achieving worldly success – why doesn't it automatically produce the happiness and fulfilment we've been promised?

I've become convinced that the two issues are interdependent: if we function by using everything we do as an attempt to distract ourselves from our mortality, we can gain financial reward but cannot live a fully satisfying life because at some level we still intuit that we're living a lie - even in our sanitised lives Death is always waiting in the wings. It is this very self-deception that undermines any hope of achieving the necessary sense of authentic purpose and meaning we so crave. This in turn further fuels our headless chicken routines as each dream bursts like a child's bubble when captured; rather than providing us with the joy that comes from feeling we're 'in the flow', in the right place and at the right time to make the most of opportunities as they present.

Put simply, if we focus primarily on the physical, do our best to repress mental and emotional discomfort, then our spiritual needs don't even make it onto the radar.

But what happens if in fact, we've got the cart before the horse?

> Let us consider a paradox: it could be that we are not so much human beings who may choose to walk a spiritual path, but rather spiritual beings who have chosen to walk a human path

What Patrick MacManaway then goes on to say captures the premise that I plan to explore:

> From this perspective, health may be seen as the acceptance and expression of our uniqueness. Part of a process of reaching a state of greater self-acceptance and self-expression is learning to trust the inner self and to receive its wisdom. This wise self knows who we are and what we need and will bring us towards ever greater experiences of joy and peace. This joy and peace is the reality of the balanced interaction between body, mind and spirit.
>
> (Dowsing for Health Dr Patrick MacManaway   2002)

This is the crux:

- are we so divorced from the self-evident benefits of this inner guide that we need to re-learn how to access and, most of all, to act on it?

- is it however possible that the process of dying actually open us to levels of this spiritual awareness that give depth and meaning as we take stock of our lives?

- even as we're forced by ill-health to pare down our outward activities, are we still learning and growing, immeasurably enriched by what onlookers can only perceive as a series of losses?

- in turn, do the insights we gain from the appreciation of a life well lived, make it more likely that we will achieve 'a good death', having used them to lay to rest the hurts and hurting we've experienced?

If, as I'm starting to sense, the entire universe is interconnected, then simply by 'being the change' perhaps I can inspire more people to embrace their dying? Rather than viewing the so-called negative emotions of sadness at loss, rage and fear at the apparent unfairness and arbitrariness of lives seemingly cut short; can we switch to seeing them as mere storm clouds that are as much a part of the cycle of growth as the sunshine and flowers? Will this then provide a means of naming and cherishing our experiences of the mystical that arise during this process and in so doing, encourage us to embrace our innate spirituality?

My hope therefore is that by charting my own journey, what is written here will go some way towards providing a language to communicate what is essentially intangible, yet is as valid as what we can discern with our five physical senses. If we can each of us, individually, change our mind-set about Life and Death, will we be freed to live our lives to the maximum and die when our natural time has arrived? In turn will this allow our passing to be with the grace and dignity that inspires and hopefully offers some small consolation for those we leave behind?

The alternative is a self-reinforcing cycle where, by paying equal attention to our physical, emotional, mental and spiritual well-being creates a balance that enables us to withstand 'life's slings and arrows'. When this is underpinned by an awareness (and crucially, acceptance) of our own mortality, we can live fully and die well when our time comes. Then because we have lived to be true to ourselves (to what some might term our soul's purpose), we can reap the rewards of having shared our unique gifts and achievements. Lived authentically, in this way every life from prince to pauper and irrespective of its length, has equal value.

So it may well be that it is those of us who are dying who are therefore best placed to reveal the preciousness of life – and how this in turn lays the groundwork for a good death.

My own experiences to date are certainly consistent with this - a massive learning curve, supported throughout by synchronicity and serendipity rather than my active willpower. '*it is when we are pushed to the edge of life that we see life most clearly'* (ibid)

Chapter I: Drop-off Zone

Meet me where I am

Please don't come to visit me out of a sense of duty.

"Shoulds, musts and oughts" are tyrants

that drown out the voice of our inner wisdom.

Maybe you're already spread too thin,

with your own responsibilities and preoccupations,

because "Life happens" to us all.

Please, respect this.

When you are here,

please don't treat me like an invalid –

yes, I do have a life limiting illness,

but that's still only one small part of who I am.

Where you see only losses,

Because the extent of my world has shrunk to a few rooms;

I'm learning first-hand that Nature abhors a vacuum

and so my spiritual life has blossomed

into this newly available space.

So I need you to be authentic: share but don't burden;

listen for the meaning behind my words,

as I will to yours.

When we have Trust,

then any Fears, Anger and Grief

will dissolve in this sacred space created by our time together.

Leaving us to share in the Ultimate:

the Gifts of the Spirit.

Chris Braithwaite

To start at the beginning.

(11th January 2016) Yes, I AM dying.

No, this is not a problem for me – I think of it more as a graduation ceremony, a "lifetime's achievement" award, before moving on to whatever lies ahead. So I'm sorry that, given all the implications, it's not an easy statement to process.

Yes, the benefits are humungous; not least because this foreknowledge gives me chance to say proper goodbyes. And if, in doing so, it helps family and friends challenge the current misconceptions about the end of life, then so much the better.

No, I don't currently have a medical diagnosis confirming this. But I do have the inner wisdom to map the tipping point that occurred last June. Illustrated by the realisation that now I'm living through the inexorable process of being forced to physically / emotionally let go of much of what was entailed in daily life. "Win – Win" however, as I discover that, this creates the space I will need for the more spiritual preoccupations which go towards creating a "good" death.

I'm not being a hypochondriac and it's certainly not some intellectual bid to impose control in the face of uncertainty. Instead, as a Quaker I know how *way opens'* – with amazing, even bizarre series of "coincidences", that disclose unlooked for, but nevertheless welcome, opportunities. All associated with increased energy for creativity as the clutter of preconceptions, as much as physical "stuff", are shed. But with them, a simultaneous reduction in core vitality as my "get up and go" wanes perceptibly. This is fine too, because as Quakers we're also encouraged to listen for the promptings of that inner *'still, small voice of calm'*, which inevitably gets clearer as the ever-present white noise distractions fade. So, though my appetite is erratic and I'm needing lots more sleep, it's easy to trust with Julian of Norwich that "*all shall be well and all will be well and all manner of things shall be well*" (Collected works)

The challenge therefore is actually to stay open to the possibility that I also may be mistaken. To acknowledge the cautions from friends who fear that I'm "writing myself off" and accepting that, yes "a little learning is a dangerous thing". In putting 1 and 1 together I may indeed be coming up with conclusions a long way off the mark. All the time being gentle with them, knowing they see me through mists of their own losses and pain. But the biggest challenge, whilst I'm progressing through the gate keeping system from GP, to consultant, to tests and finally meeting with the specialist; is to "walk alongside" my husband – the person who has to endure the same uncertainty, but at some point come to terms with being the one who will be left behind after a marriage that has spanned 3 decades.

* * * *

Dying – the final frontier?

So, maybe nothing's changed that much? But it does seem that the medicalisation of death has moved the dying away from all that is familiar, onto hospital wards or into hospices; to experience the inevitable loss of dignity involved in what Bowlby, in a different context, criticised as "stranger care in a group setting". In turn, our families have been deskilled since the "battle" is too often to exercise technological or pharmaceutical prowess in order to preserve life at any cost, without factoring in the resultant quality of life.

Talk to paramedics and you'll realise fear of litigation means they'll work for half an hour to resuscitate a man despite his inoperable brain tumour. Apparently it doesn't even count if you've gone to the pain and expense of having DNR ("Do not resuscitate") tattooed in all the colours of the rainbow across your chest – they have to consider that you may have changed your mind in the interim!

Plus, despite the reassurance offered by the Hippocratic oath that doctors each take to "do no harm", it turns out that it isn't nearly so easy to apply in real life. My Dad died on a hospital ward having had a move to residential care denied as a result of contracting MRSA. He was already 2 pyjama sizes larger than normal because the effect of his medication had upset the chemicals that regulate water balance. All this happened after he'd undergone 2 operations because the first surgeon had discovered that the tumour to be excised was a few inches lower than expected, so wasn't within his remit. And despite the family spending his remaining 3 days pleading for him to be transferred to the local hospice, this was refused "because he might last for months yet". (I know now much has changed in the care of the dying as my own experiences have since demonstrated, however at the commencement of my writing this is how things were.)

But the approach I chose isn't a cheap excuse to rant against the short comings of orthodox approaches. Nor can it be a "one size fits all" panacea. It's more of an experiment to discover whether there might be an alternative for a better death.

So what would I see as a good death?

I seem to recall that the Buddha transcended whilst sitting in the shade of a Banyan tree, which feels suitably risk free. But there's a definite shortage of these on the Isle of Wight – and it would take a crash course in spirituality and/or quantum physics for me to know how to affect such a shift between worlds.

Pain free would be ideal, but not at the expense of lucidity unless the pain becomes unbearable.

Slipping away during sleep might be traumatic for those who try to rouse me, unless it's part of an already established illness such as pneumonia, known in the past with good reason as "*the old man's friend*".

Maybe simply not coming out from an anaesthetic – though there would have to have been a prior injunction for the medics to not apply "heroic measures".

In their small booklet with a big WOW! factor that prompts us to consider to what degree our lives are an expression of the 5 testimonies, Quakers ask... *Are you able to contemplate your death and the death of those closest to you?* (because in) *Accepting the fact of death, we are freed to live more fully.* (Quaker Advices & Queries #30)

This makes absolute sense to me because intuitively it feels that unless we pay attention to how transient the individual experiences are that accumulate to form Life, I can't see how we can revel in the full wonder of what it means to be here at this specific point in time and space. Otherwise, as John Lennon famously sang (taking the quote from Alan Saunders 1957 Readers Digest quote) to his *Beautiful Boy*: "*Life is what happens to you when you're busy making other plans*". It would, after all, be as strange to require that we always enjoy sunshine, without appreciating the respite that darkness provides or the riches that rainfall releases.

Interestingly, a few years ago when I thought we were going to be forced to sell up, I was grief stricken at the prospect of losing our organic veg patch, stunning views and wonderful neighbours. Yet, what I'm now discovering is effectively a total change of perspective; an almost palpable excitement that having "*done that and got the T shirt for good measure*", the opportunity to move on is as exciting as packing for (what is literally) the "trip of a lifetime".

There is of course the pull of attachments but I'm with Richard Bach on this:

Don't be

dismayed at good-byes.

A farewell is necessary before

you can meet

again.

And meeting

again, after moments or

lifetimes, is certain for

those who are

friends

(*Illusions – the adventures of a reluctant messiah – Richard Bach*)

Then what about the attachment to life itself, that seems to cause many to linger? Sometimes it's to see a child graduate or a grandchild born and therefore clearly life enhancing for all concerned. But in other cases, there's what seems at least to bystanders to be simply a hanging on, in a not quite dead limbo. Maybe the pull of hurts that needed resolving or resentments harboured, can prevent a more timely exit? Or could it be there are processes at work that we simply can't detect with any of our state of the art monitors?

One suggestion is that as well as *approach*(ing) *old age with courage and hope* we should, *as far as possible, make arrangements for our care in good time, so that an undue burden does not fall on others* (Quakers A&Q #29) But this raises the question of what constitutes an "undue burden"? My sister and I for instance were in our early thirties when we nursed our mother for the final month of her life. And it's something I wouldn't wish on my worst enemy! Despite the skill and compassion of a small team of Macmillan nurses billeted with us for the duration, we watched her deteriorate until we were praying each night for her release.

In fact, she died precisely as she lived, frequently taking the opposite course to what was in her best interests. Not in an altruistic way but as a feisty northern woman, desperate to assert her identity when feeling lost in her marriage and overwhelmed by motherhood. As a result we stood impotently by for too many days as she apparently died from starvation. We did what we felt "good daughters should", completely unaware that the flashbacks would haunt our dreams for years; or that, for over a decade, the coming of Spring would be marred by the echoes of memories that had burned into our beings at a cellular level, of the bleak dread of what new horrors each new day would reveal.

As Blake Morrison captures in the title of the book recounting his own experience, it's a case of "*And when did you last see your father*"; because the unique spark that makes them who they are seems long-since extinguished, though the heart carries on beating in a seemingly empty husk. Other friends, similarly traumatised, make the point that if it were a pet, the RSPCA would long ago have intervened to put an end to the unnecessary suffering. It's hardly surprising that my father sought to protect us from this, stoically enduring the progressive erosion of dignity on a frantically paced surgical ward.

And is a "good" death even achievable?

With the best will in the world, there are inherent problems within the western orthodox approach to healthcare that can create significant obstacles to dying well. I've spent most of my working life trying to join the dots and grapple with the contradictions:

- if we accept the premise that disease is pathological and can only be cured by experts, then we are required to abdicate responsibility for our own health and well-being. This essentially makes us victims: let down by our own bodies and therefore doubly dependent on "specialists" with their access to technology →

- this effectively imbues medics with the role of Hero, battling to save us in the face of adversity; but crucially, denying them the psychological support for times when interventions don't work and they "fail" →

- my sense is that most medics are therefore not only affected by largely unrecognised post-traumatic shock disorder; but also, in order to survive, will have to harden themselves to their patient's distress by focussing on the "task", which merely serves to suppress rather than cure symptoms

The irony is that having "signed on" to alleviate suffering, they are effectively complicit in causing it, because what we as patients tend to overlook is that every intervention inevitably involves some level of invasiveness or trade off with unwanted effects of drugs. Factor in to this the stress and resultant exhaustion that is the experience of healthcare workers, along with the bottom-line priorities of the multi-national pharmaceutical companies.

Ben Goldacre's *Bad Pharma* for instance makes for shocking reading in listing the "dirty tricks" employed to maintain shareholder dividends at the expense of both the NHS and its patients. It's hardly surprising that patients are caught between the proverbial rock and hard place.

Edward Whitmont, Jungian therapist wrote:

> *A great healer once remarked that "a physician never enters a sick room alone, but is always accompanied by a host of angels or demons". Whether the healer comes with angels or demons will be determined by the degree of the healer's conscious awareness of his own wounds and impulses toward wounding and by his ability to process them, to potentise them to their symbolic*

essence and hence not to be carried away by them nor to project (and projectively induce) them in his patients. (Whitmont *The Alchemy of Healing* p.200)

If we then introduce the "Big C" into the equation, with all the associated media fuelled images of waging war against cancer, Fear becomes a virtual entity. It pressures all concerned to react swiftly and decisively (compounded by the omnipresent shadow of litigation)

- by focussing on the offending symptoms however, each individual is reduced to an object, depersonalised and even institutionalised by their very desire to comply in order to be seen as a *"good patient"*   →

- where the focus is on symptom management, those who then *"fail to respond to treatment"* describe the abandonment they experience after the dreaded words that *"nothing further can be done"*; particularly when palliative services are not immediately required   →

- worse still, having already been disempowered by this process, they are less likely to be able to access their own inner healing powers; much less understand that change is required at an infinitely more profound level than for example removing the tumour, in order to effect a lasting cure →

- moreover, their inner wisdom has been deeply discomforted by the real life experience of the profound mismatch between the stated benevolence of the medical intention and the reality of institutional health care. It is tragic to hear the majority of patients who therefore resort to blaming themselves for their inability to get well, hypnotised by the illusion of an apparently omnipotent technological regimen.

But what if dying (just as pregnancy for that matter) is not a pathological process, but rather a natural evolution with its own stages and rhythms? Then a model that is geared to preserving life at all cost is simply not applicable. Such a mechanistic approach is fine as an analogy if we are taking our car to be serviced, but entirely inadequate if what we understand as "health" is actually to be defined as far more than by simply "the absence of disease".

Instead I would suggest that what is needed is a suitably comprehensive approach that factors in the complex interplay of mind and body, spiritual and emotional needs. This will enable us to get to know ourselves again and in so doing, to regain our trust in the complex interplay of bodily systems that have, after all, evolved over eons to ensure the survival of human-kind. By taking back responsibility for our own health in this way we give due respect to our uniqueness, restore our own faith in the validity of our senses and realise that we always have choices that enable us, if we pay careful attention, to navigate by means of our own "inner wisdom".

We can also remind ourselves that thanks to the ease of world-wide communication, we in the West now have access to an infinite variety of health care traditions from civilisations that existed long before our own. Each has its own model for restoring balance by means of forms of physical cleansing as in detoxification. But where they differ from the western model is that they also give equal weight to more esoteric forms of purification, in recognition of the inextricable link between our spiritual well-being and our general health.

Western mechanistic approaches certainly have their place IF we have access to reliable data by which to gauge their true effectiveness. In fact as research by the College of Medicine shows repeatedly, by restricting their use to these specific situations and then incorporating practices such as acupuncture which has proven effectiveness for instance in the management of pain, we see vastly improved patient outcomes. Otherwise, it's a case of "if the only tool in your belt is a hammer, you have to treat everything as a nail"

* * * *

"Inner wisdom"

What does it take to (re)learn how to listen to this inner wisdom?

First I'd suggest we need to rewrite the script that says that we're falling apart if we fail to function at 110%, 24/7! As I discovered when recovering from a decade suffering with Chronic Fatigue Syndrome it's impossible to pay attention to our true physical needs if we're zombified by sleep deprivation, regularly reduced to crying jags or homicidal rage, or feeling light headed and nauseous as a result of caffeine or sugar-induced highs and lows.

After a generation of being conditioned to be high achievers however, I suspect I'm not alone in needing to be actively given permission to be more realistic about the demands we place on ourselves. In fact most computers would have crashed long ago under the pressure involved in a pace of life that now requires we juggle work, home, family and social commitments without respite!

To spell it out therefore, respecting our basic needs means:

- adequate sleep and regular digestion - essential for the physiological fuelling, repair and nourishment of all our systems

- stabilising mood swings by selecting low glycaemic (slow release sugar) snacks and eating meals in peace, away from the office desk or TV

- controlling blood pressure levels by recognising and then addressing stressors: building on emotional literacy, employing anger management techniques , implementing relaxation strategies, taking breaks from the agitation-inducing computer games

We'll then have the energy to exercise regularly, releasing the feel-good hormones that help keep us motivated; rather than vegging-out in front of various screens, subconsciously absorbing all manner of negative images.

Secondly, in order to simply be able to hear any inner voice, we need to turn down the volume of the attention-seeking screams of panic, triggered by misinterpreting basic data. To this end it's immensely helpful to get familiar with the signs for instance that the immune system is functioning healthily. When we recognise that discharges/nausea + vomiting, inflammation (particularly swollen glands) and temperature fluctuations are perfectly natural, they'll no longer elicit the knee jerk GP's appointment for expert reassurance nor the expectation of medication as a quick fix.

In fact, it was a real eye opener for me to discover these symptoms are simply signs that the immune system has dispatched fighter cells to the site of the infection and they're generating some heat and swelling in the process of disposing of the bacteria, viruses – or dodgy food! So rather than trying to carry on regardless, I came to accept that a twice yearly flush out of some description involving 3 days of rest, adequate amounts of fluids and general self-care, can only optimise performance. Such a relief after viewing anything other than perfection as being a sign of weakness and definitely a case for working smarter, not harder!

Thirdly, despite the fact that the sentiment has been cheapened by being hi-jacked by beauty ads, we need to trust that we are "worth it". Worthy of the good things that will happen if we follow our true instincts, to get off the treadmill of putting the needs of others above our own and confront the guilt that apparently "being selfish" elicits. Our aim is for balance: between work, rest and play, plus giving and receiving care; so that we meet our physical, emotional, mental and spiritual needs.

Effectively it's another set of "permissions" that not only actively encourage us to avoid the drains on energy which characterise vampire-type relationships or no-win scenarios; but builds the resilience that helps us bounce back when inevitably "Life happens". At a head level, awareness of the 4P's (protective, precipitating, predisposing and perpetuating factors) that either work in our favour or act as an Achilles heel, means that we are then better equipped to respond appropriately rather than react unhelpfully when faced with challenges. Otherwise, not only are we running on empty, but because our adrenal system has yet to evolve to deal with constant stress, there is increasing likelihood of it behaving erratically; with for example anxiety/panic attacks, signs that it's flooding our system.

After these basics, the rest is pretty much "cherry on the cake". When we've stopped over-riding our body's "warning systems" and eat nutritious food when we're hungry, rest when we're tired and avoid the constant over-stimulation of being plugged into various IT tools; we've taken the first crucial, though undoubtedly hardest, steps.

It is this that helps us recognise that we all do indeed possess a fully functioning internal guide, whether we name it gut instinct or bull shit *(B.S)* detector! Then, when we're no longer poised for fight or flight, we can start to take the risk of hearing what it has to say, without dreading that we might be overwhelmed. At this point, paying attention to indicators of imbalance becomes progressively easier since we quickly learn it pays massive dividends in terms of feeling happier, more in control and therefore capable of sustaining satisfying relationships.

What is even more exciting, is that it enriches our lives exponentially because those around us step up, inspired that they too can enjoy the fruits of this great energy. As it says in Marianne Williamson's often quoted *"Our deepest Fear"*

> *We are all meant to shine as children do. We were born to manifest the glory that is within us. It's not*

just in some of us, it's in everyone. And as we let our own light shine, we unconsciously give other people permission to do the same. As we're liberated from our own fear, our presence automatically liberates others.

Any change however is a challenge, because it involves letting go of what no longer fits, but is oh so comfortable in its familiarity! I vividly recall a tutor demonstrating this process by clinging to the arms of his chair, illustrating how finally it is pure exhaustion that prevents us carrying on. So it's kinder on ourselves (and those around us) if we can spot the build-up before we burn out, collapse or experience any other form of break down.

At the very least, if we are unprepared for an inevitable period of discomfort, we are less likely to persist and more inclined to sink into passivity or rail against forces outside ourselves. So yes, it is always the first step that is the hardest – but, once we have learned to walk, we can become, if not athletes precisely, certainly a lot closer to making best use of all those physical and mental muscles that enable us to achieve our full potential.

* * * *

Mysticism – our sixth sense

Once we are "in the zone" therefore we clearly know it because paradoxically actions require significantly less effort. "Coincidences" abound that bring the kind of unlikely openings that would be dismissed as too far-fetched if they were a plot line in fiction. We achieve a state of calm alertness, confident that simply by paying attention we'll be nudged onwards, rather than repeatedly colliding with dead ends. Although I only get glimpses of what it's like to "sit lightly" with events whilst they unfold, it's been enough to confirm the advantages of stopping striving or worse, fretting over what can't be changed.

This laying down of burdens however is far more than passive fatalism and closer to the depiction of a Zen-like state. I don't subscribe to god-language but increasingly use the phrase *"thy will be done"* to hand issues over to the universe (or whatever you term the greater being) particularly when faced with the pains of those around me that no words can soothe.

> *Do you try to set aside times of quiet for openness to the Holy Spirit? All of us need to find a way into silence which allows us to deepen our awareness of the divine and to find the inward source of our strength. Seek to know an inward stillness, even*

amid the activities of daily life

[Advices & Queries #3]

Then once we have learned to switch off the incessant chatter of external demands and discovered a point of stillness where we allow ourselves to be open to all possibilities, we move from needing the "99% perspiration" to get jobs done.

This automatically makes more space for "inspiration", where we learn consciously how to harness the way that ego dissolves during any act of creation, so that we access something beyond and greater than our physical selves to inform our choices....which is where the magic starts.

When we unleash our unique creativity it is like being given permission to stop pushing at a door that opens inwards and just getting out of the way! The relief that comes from this resulting change in perspective is tangible and what was previously seen as "problem solving" is opened up to the inspiration that comes from - if not exactly seeing the big picture - at least knowing that we are part of one.

Spiritual learning continues throughout life, and often in unexpected ways. There is inspiration to be found all around us, in the natural world, in the

science and arts, in our work and friendships, in
our sorrows as well as in our joys. Are you open to
new light, from whatever source it may come? Do
you approach new ideas with discernment?
[Advices & Queries #7]

As the above highlights however, this requires that we tread a fine line: to be "open" to the riches inherent in such insights, especially when they barrel down on us unexpectedly (in the launderette for instance rather than a more explicitly spiritual setting); and yet, to remain vigilant and cautious so that we avoid being blown off course by simply chasing each latest trend.

If, as I suspect, all that I am describing here could be viewed as mystical communion, the challenge therefore is how to express in words?

Since this is new ground for me I have reproduced a list of features compiled by Peter and Elizabeth Fenwick in their *The truth in the light,* because their research into Near Death Experiences (NDE) provided some useful benchmarks correlating features that are consistently reported as being associated with mystical experiences. It is the first time I've come across such a comprehensive list, so I was doubly surprised to see how well it fits with my own experiences. My hope therefore is that it will provide a shared language by which, as a total novice, I can attempt to find ways as these musings progress, to articulate both the credibility and validity of the deeply moving insights that have been and will continue to be, my trusty guides over these coming months.

Mystical Experiences

1. *An intense realness*

   It comes with the conviction of absolute truth, so the experiencer is overcome by the validity and meaning of the experience

2. *Feelings of unity*

   The experiencer feels (s)he has seen through to the fundamental nature of the universe, perceives and understands it and is united with it

3. *A feeling that the experience is 'ineffable'*

   There are no words to describe it. All sensory experiences would fall into this category if language did not contain words to describe it. As soon as some new or unusual sensation is experienced, then it becomes ineffable

4. *Transcendence of space and time* For me *it* may be as simple the feeling of de-ja-vue, a dream of a snatched future moment, the certainty of somehow knowing that stranger or even the get together with

a long lost old friend and picking us as if it were only yesterday

5. *A sense of sacredness* for me it has come from walking into that wooded grove and simply feeling the wonder being generated all around in the near silent, misty morning as shafts of light cut through the canopy

6. *Deeply felt positive mood* - Feelings of joy and peace and contentment – for me looking at the face of the sleeping child as the smile on my face touches my heart at the serenity of the moment or catching the look of love on my partners face as I wake

7. *Paradoxicality* - The feeling that something which is 'impossible' is in fact possible

8. *Transiency* – may be good things that seem to be over too quickly or moving swiftly on; passing through

9. *Positive changes in attitude and behaviour*

I find it particularly helpful the writers point out that none of these is unique to the mysticism associated with spirituality: being common for instance in the near death experiences they were researching, as well as in many drug-induced states, the experience of being in love, reported by people with epilepsy (as a precursor to an attack) and quite often occurring in athletes during and after great performances. And from my own experiences I take this to mean that a) thankfully we don't have to wait for an NDE in order to get a sense of mystical communion and b) such incidents are much more widely experienced than we might realise. In fact the authors noted an almost universal reluctance to be seen as "wacky", which had inhibited test subjects from disclosing these life enhancing experiences until they were encouraged to do so by participating in the study.

Another of the many gifts I have received since starting these musings is a growing appreciation of the connection that links creativity with the act of worship. Since attending Quaker meetings where those present sit mainly in silence, without hymns or prayers and with no priest figure to intercede on our behalf, I have given a great deal of thought to their dynamics. It is an entirely different experience than being part of a congregation, being led through a programmed service.

There is also a different energy between for instance meditation and Quaker worship, only partly due to taking part within a group setting. In fact, especially whilst I was still working full-time and had been reluctant to give up my Sunday morning commune with nature achieved by gardening; I little realised that just as *the whole is bigger than the parts*, an hour spent engaged with others in actively listening for promptings (of Spirit?) can produce a sense of creative vibrancy totally at odds with the bored silences that we mostly endure.

This essentially private experience of mine was given voice by Julia Cameron in *Walking in this world - practical strategies for creativity*.

> *'We are made by the great Creator and are intended to be creative ourselves. As we seek to co-operate with that intention, the still, small voice that all spiritual paths speak of becomes an ever more present reality. When we go within there is someone or something there to meet us and it is not mute to our identity'* (p.39)

In a similar vein in *The vision of the fool and other writings* by artist-writer Cecil Collins, declares that,

> *'art is a metaphysical activity... that has at its purpose to evoke that inexplicable, numinous power which is the mysterious unity of life'*

Both are confident that irrespective of levels of artistic ability we can all *connect with inspiration and your inner creative spirit* because when we make space to "stand and stare" we are freed to make more profound connections with the surrounding world. Then literally anything can trigger this awe inspiring sense a mystic communion: from the breath-taking sense of being a part in the rich cosmic tapestry achieved whether worshipping alone or in Meeting; to the profound satisfaction of seeing something as mundane as a draining rack of clean plates and glassware refracting rainbows of light across the kitchen.

Thanks also to the pioneering work of neuroscientists and associated professionals, we are now discovering ways of harnessing this same creative process to safely access aspects hidden deep in our unconscious and hence bring into awareness material that is invaluable in improving our daily living.

It seems that just like the monsters under the bed, most fears, griefs and anger can be defused by shining a metaphorical light on them, freeing us to feel the one remaining emotion, which is the joy that is liberated when our creativity takes flight.

Although for those addicted to the messaging that involves constant distractions and interruptions, it may take a leap of faith to step into this stillness and trust that any promptings that arise from this place will not only be in our best interests, but help us make choices that have been informed by a much deeper wisdom than simple intellect!

As an example of the thinness of the veil that exists between conscious and unconscious worlds, in *the Secret world of Drawings* Gregg Furth presents case studies that challenge our rational understanding. He illustrates how the drawings made by adults and children alike reveal, not only an apparently impossible level of insight into the physical and emotional symptoms they are currently experiencing, but in some cases actually predict these months before diagnosis.

Since his book was based on the research undertaken for his doctoral thesis and 16 years of work in this field, it provides unambiguous evidence that with the simple tools of paper and a few pencils or crayons we can all access and place our faith in both the existence and credibility of such a guide.

Then of course, the more we access it the more we can trust that our intuition is a reliable indicator and we can gradually get back to the point where we can acknowledge that we are each the expert when it comes to knowing ourselves right through to the most profound level of our beings.

Listening to our inner wisdom

I'm fond of the maxim that having been given 2 ears and 1 mouth, we should employ them accordingly and spend twice as much time listening as we do talking. Yet instead, I am only too aware of the great many strategies I indulge in when I'm avoiding listening to others – particularly my husband – mea-culpa! (Sorry R) So it is hardly surprising that when it comes to listening to my inner wisdom, it can take a crisis and the ensuing desperation to drive me to tune in to the promptings that are otherwise drowned out by the everyday static.

> ... the skill of **listening**: listening not just to the words, but to the feelings and needs behind the words. It takes a great deal of time and energy to listen well. It's a kind of weaving: reflecting back, asking for clarification, asking for time in turn to be listened to, being truly open to what we're hearing (even if it hurts), being open to the possibility that we might ourselves be changed by what we hear.
> (Mary Lou Leavitt *Quaker Faith & Practice* #20.71)

This is a far cry from the verbal wrestling that more typically occurs to dominate the air space; when so-called conversational "exchanges" revert to monologues with each party talking with little reference to the others, just as toddlers play alongside rather than with each other.

Yet I am discovering even the potential of having a life limiting illness is an opportunity to undertake a crash course in valuing intuition – like regularly taking my own pulse for clues about what is likely to be the least damaging course to achieve the best possible outcome and being open to the existence of resources that are available to me. It certainly helps me stay focused in the present moment rather than screaming under the weight of "what ifs".

I have also discovered how many myths and prejudices get in the way of my being heard in turn by those who can no longer see me behind the diagnosis of terminal illness. They share the common but misguided desire to remain "positive" despite prognoses or to pitch in with non-relevant experiences or advice. It has required much tenderness therefore to do what seems to be counter-intuitive and actually name rather than deny a distress. An even more insidious dynamic is the "invitation" to buy into playing the victim by accepting the role of the invalid, by which I risk becoming the focus of horrified pity, rather than empowered to draw on the innate resilience that has helped me bounce back in the past. All these temptations get run past my trusty "B-S" detector and amazingly this has always defused its power, both for me and those involved.

It is of course even more important to be able to mine these riches for those around me, who are dealing with a completely different set of unknowns: the shock of anticipated loss, compounded by the appalling sense of impotence at being bystanders in an unfolding drama. When I ask my husband if, given the enormity of everything we are facing, the calm acceptance that results from my regular submersion in silent retreat from the world seems somehow insulting, his reply is always an emphatic denial. In fact the reverse is true - he draws strength from my conviction that there is something bigger at play that I am clearly accessing, that he in turn can benefit from even though it is a complete anathema to him.

The challenge of acting on our inner wisdom

Making room in our lives to allow our inner wisdom the opportunity to be expressed, be it directly in words or through subconscious routes such as our creativity or dreams, is actually however only half of the equation. I certainly find it equally challenging to then pay attention, let alone act on, what I'm hearing! There are the tired excuses, citing the fear of the hurt that I might cause, or the anger or disapproval that might be provoked; rather than facing the discomfort involved in making the changes that I know only too well are long overdue.

Worse still I have found that in common with a great many others, the fear of being seen to be "wacky" has held me back from rising to the challenge of discovering ways to communicate what feels to be both intensely private and precious. I am therefore indebted to those I have met who have been prepared to talk openly about "the spooky stuff".

So it feels appropriate at this point to test the water and put aside my embarrassment in order to bear witness to my experiences in the early weeks; when both friends and strangers upheld us through the uncertain times in their various ways, according to their beliefs, skills and resources. The following are examples...

- candles lit in Liverpool, Lincoln and Chester cathedrals

- prayers said on our behalf by congregations and healing groups, though we will never get to know, least of all to thank them in person

- different forms of energy healing – both remote and in person

- generosity of spirit in the willingness to respect our decisions as being right for us and recognising that we are indeed "fighting" but on our own terms, despite having simultaneously to process the shock of our news and its implications

- multiple acts of kindness in taking the time out of already busy lives: to send cards, emails, letters - each expressing sentiments direct from the heart; to phone or drop by in person bringing fresh flowers and assorted thoughtful treats; to share meals and, weather permitting even walks with us

- in the absence of immediate family, the commitment to sign up to be on my "transition team": supporting the hospice palliative care team in responding both to my needs even to the point of personal care, as well as recognising the power of vigils in upholding the emotional and spiritual needs of all concerned

For anyone feeling impotent when faced with such devastating news from a friend or family member, please be assured that as the above shows, it is less what is done and by far the generosity of the intention to walk alongside, that is conveyed in any of these apparently simple acts.

The outcome has been so far beyond a purely psychological, placebo type comforting. There is the tangible warmth of being bathed in unconditional love, which is present even when I'm woken by pain. It is also evidenced by the depth and quality of the spiritual insights that arise spontaneously in what could otherwise be the darkest hours. These produce a serenity that is SO at odds with my typically frenetic approach to life, replacing it with a state of euphoria that comes from seeing everything as if through fresh eyes.

Comparing this with the "what is mystical" check list:

1. *An intense realness* – despite the culturally induced terror of '*the big C'*, R and I have already sensed the existence of strengths to draw on that have been entirely beyond our own resources. This has to be the case otherwise we would have collapsed under the enormity of it all! Instead I know absolutely that I / we will find from somewhere the capacity to deal with whatever lies ahead

2. *Feelings of unity* - rather than being overwhelmed by loneliness, 4 am seems a wonderful time to connect with the rhythms of the universe when the chatter of millions of psyches have been stilled by sleep and I can *hold in the Light* others whose needs are just as pressing, as well as "know" that I too am held

3. *A feeling that the experience is 'ineffable'* – words are either too clumsy when it comes to trying to convey the profound, almost child-like comfort that comes from a sense of being safely enveloped; or have cringe-making associations so that feeling "blissed out" makes it easier for me to question the impact of the pain killers rather than trust that this could be valid

4. *Transcendence of space and time* – there are so many occasions when it feels as if I'm outside, looking in, that this is not happening to the "real" me. Instead there is a sense of the surreal, as if a parallel universe is operating from which an infinite number of paths diverge, a playful setting where different sets of outcomes can be selected to satisfy soul's purpose

5. *A sense of sacredness* – for me this doesn't have any religious connotations but is nevertheless as breathtakingly awe-invoking as all of creation. But with it the sense of a desperately fragile purity that is vulnerable to intellectual and ego-centric behaviours

6. *Deeply felt positive mood* – this is different from "happiness" because it is sustained even when all seems bleak and unendurable. Perhaps this is what is meant by "faith" since it runs counter to conditioning??

7. *Paradoxicality* – this entire experience defies logic and flies in the face of conventional wisdom because despite the implicit tragedy I truly feel blessed to be receiving the gifts it contains

8. *Transiency* – although the resulting insights burn as briefly and unexpectedly as sparks from a fire, the memory of them remains and is as warming even after they have long gone

9. *Positive changes in attitude and behaviour* – more than simply *'nothing to lose, everything to gain'* and closer to the way that good friends elicit the best in us

And because she says it so much better than I possibly could, I am concluding with this statement by Margaret Silf (*Faith* Darton, Longman & Todd Ltd 2011)

There is a big divide between people who regard life as a random event in a random universe, with no inherent meaning, and those who believe that their life's journey, and the journey of all humanity, has real meaning and purpose. Perhaps there is no answer. But to be a person of faith is to come down on the side of meaning. And our deep desire to discover meaning in life might in itself be a sign that there is meaning to be discovered ... to really satisfy our heart's searching, to be truly convinced ... perhaps we

need to search our own experience first, because any sense
of purpose will be personal, before it becomes universal

I am clearly, not only in the "meaning camp" but also faced with the question of whether I believe the universe to be ultimately benevolent, neutral or hostile towards us, am convinced that despite all the problems life has and will continue to pose, there is a Grand Plan. My sense is that this is about learning to recognise and share our Spirit Given Gifts for the benefit of all, but mostly, for ourselves.

*   *   *   *

And so it comes full circle: without doubt, back in June when I started to notice subtle changes in intensity, duration and frequency of symptoms; paid attention to the resulting physiological changes and recognised the potential that it might indicate a life limiting illness…..

……I was not losing the plot!!

Increasingly, when I day dream…

…my in and out breaths have created an almost tangible sense of being rocked by the motion of a small boat as it makes its way along a river, at a speed that provides ample opportunity to focus on the minutiae. Time: to revel in the birdsong; the play of sunlight on water; the shape and texture of the clouds skating equally lazily across the sky. There's an evocative mix of loam and wood smoke that drifts with the haze across from the surrounding fields, as the seasonal cycle continues and harvest stubble is ploughed in. Mostly though, it's the glorious technicolour effect, with all the trees that we pass beneath shedding their leaves in a way that seems to paint the whole world in real and refracted gold.

Then, imperceptibly at first, the flood plains were replaced by rolling hills until, without warning, the river was slicing deep below limestone cliffs, their majesty too high for direct sunlight to penetrate. There was a notable shift too: a fresher air quality, plus a quickening sense of purpose to what had hitherto simply felt like "time out" and a welcome reminder of Gaia's abundance.

Now of course, true to archetype, we're travelling through subterranean caverns. Initially there were the exposed, arm-sized roots of centuries old trees, weathered to a patina that suggests eons of sentient touch. Then we moved deeper, to the same millstone grit revealed on the surface by dynamiting only a generation earlier, when roads were being gouged through the North Staffs Moorland. Slabs of rock, the size of buildings and the colour of dried blood shot through with the sparkle of quartz.

From time to time the tunnels widen to reveal an embankment, sometimes on our left, more frequently on our right, where footprints in the mud reveal that 2, or more-likely 4 legged creatures continue to follow the course of the river. I think, maybe wishfully that I see badgers, the successors of all those who have gone before, working in harmony after the Ice Age river had gouged its way through the soft rock, to raise their young safe from human persecution.

Though the depth of the surrounding darkness is now absolute and the cold as petrifying as the stalagmites growing ever upwards, there is a soft light and warmth that emanates from the boat. I'm also aware of a figure behind me, occasionally correcting our course as we disregard the openings of certain tunnels in order to follow our own trajectory. He (I'm sure he's male, but here to offer his strength only for protection) is cloaked in feathers? Skins? that are striped in black and grey-white. My badger totem? A reminder of my fascination with tales of South American shamans, transcending the corporeal and effecting healing by divining what to Western ideology we deem the DNA helix, but they understand as 2 inter-coiled snakes, reminiscent of the caduceus.

To complete our group of travellers, we're joined by the yellow-eyed eagle that had gazed imperiously as we'd passed, from the massive fir standing in grand isolation to mark the shift between worlds. Gliding on wings so wide they brushed the cavern walls, it landed, as if taking up its rightful position on the raised prow of the boat; eyes piercing into the darkness ahead and entirely indifferent to our presence.

We stand ready......

Chapter 2: Baggage check-in

Preparations

> *... the skill of **letting go**: I don't mean that in the sense of giving up, lying down and inviting people to walk all over us, but acknowledging the possibility that there may be other solutions to this ... than the ones we've thought of yet; letting the imagination in – making room for the Spirit. We need to let go of our own will – not so as to surrender to another's, but so as to look together for (God's) solution. It's a question of finding ways to let go of our commitment to opposition and separation, to letting ourselves be open to our connectedness as human beings*

> Mary Lou Leavitt 1986 (Quaker Faith & Practice #20.71)

Although strictly speaking Mary Lou Leavitt was describing the three skills (*naming, listening* and *letting go*) underpinning her strategy for managing conflict, they apply just as well to how we approach the tensions inherent in managing change. Even more so, when the temperature associated with preparing to die is ramped up into the red zone!

They interlock allowing us to weave backwards and forwards between them in response to events, so having considered "listening" in Chapter 1, we now jump ahead to "letting go" before demonstrating a strategy that shows the power involved in "naming".

Now that I've received confirmation that the hard lump in my groin is indeed a form of cancer, I'm waiting on the CT scan (3 dimensional imaging) that will show the extent of its spread and therefore indicate potential treatment options. Exactly as Mary Lou says, I can't afford to just roll over on the basis that "doctor knows best" and yet if I'm to make an informed decision ready for when I meet with the consultant, I do need to factor in the technical explanations about what the various medical procedures will entail.

This involves working through a substantial booklet put together by the Macmillan Cancer Trust. It is however filled with alien and alienating terms like canula and catheter; diagrams that in another context could be mistaken for pornography; intimidatingly detailed accounts of the different forms of treatment; plus the shocking extent of the immediate and long term impacts of any surgery / associated procedures.

Even speed reading it I can feel myself being taken over by fear of nightmarish proportions. Although good practice requires that there are designated key workers available to answer any questions, I feel too raw and fragile to ask. In reality and reflecting the dire state of the NHS, all our energy goes instead into chasing up basics such as ensuring the CT scan report will be available in time for the consultant's appointment.

The ability therefore to go deep within myself, to access what I see as my still point – the place in the river where I can stand and observe it flowing, but without risk of being swept away – means that I can remember to breathe from my abdomen (slows the release of the "fight, flight" hormone) and simply *let go*:

> of the flood of emotions that could have me wasting valuable energy ranting against the universe, blaming everything and everybody or being overwhelmed with guilt for somehow bringing this upon myself
>
> of the sadness that my world will carry on without me, particularly because having only "celebrated" my 60th birthday last May, I haven't had chance to attend to any of the projects that a planned reduction in workload could have allowed.

With each in-breath, I can feel peace washing through every cell of my body and with it an expanding awareness:

of the serendipity that has been at play to make other resources apart from the orthodox medical ones available to me

and of the synchronicity that has meant that I have friends available with the skills, shared beliefs and, most importantly, the willingness to create my own "transition team".

This is what I take to be meant by "surrender". Not the fatalistic abdication of responsibility, but rather an active trust that by getting my intellect and ego out of the equation, there is nothing to impede my inner wisdom acting in concert with the universal will. Only when these are combined can I safely navigate whatever lies ahead.

Better still, it acts like a magnet to draw to me and my situation healing energies that though they won't necessarily lead to cure, will aid in the healthy release of aspects that would otherwise hold me back. I see it very much as tapping into my creative potential and though it may seem strange to some, I feel blessed, grateful and immensely privileged to have this awareness.

Reality checks - CT scan results

Not everyone feels the same of course, but I found it immensely reassuring to read about the multi-disciplinary teams made up of, amongst others a surgeon, specialist nurse and psychologist. By working together their aim is to provide me with all the information and emotional support that will assist in making informed decisions. For me "information is power" and in any case, my imagination needs as many facts as my little grey cells can absorb to prevent it spiralling off into every parallel universe of worst case scenarios! In fact it was almost worth simultaneously smashing and dislocating my ankle 5 years ago, to have the fascinating experience of seeing the X ray showing how well the bone had fused around the metal plate. No room for misunderstanding with such unambiguous evidence.

Beware! Perhaps CT scans can't be presented in such a patient-friendly way? ... In which case we need to be forewarned! Whatever the reason, the specialist oncology surgeon charged with passing on the results decided, without even examining me, to simply list **his decisions** for treatment:

- "*radical surgery*" which, thanks only to the Macmillan information booklet, I knew was code for removing the lump itself **plus** 1 cm circumference of healthy skin surrounding it **plus** any "implicated" lymph nodes → minimum of 3 weeks hospitalisation plus extended period of bed bound convalescence due to the complexity of the surgery / follow up procedures and slow healing in that area (3 -6 months)

- an **initial** 6 course programme of chemotherapy (2 months minimum)

- followed by radiotherapy to "mop up" any remaining cancer cells → pain and scarring caused by the inevitable burns to healthy skin.

The maths for me were simple: to remove a golf ball sized growth in my groin plus a safe enough margin of healthy skin; then to blast the remainder with radiation would mean losing what my friend coyly terms her "lady parts". For someone who hadn't even endured the indignity of pregnancy and childbirth, this was a no-brainer! Duhh!!The consultant however was appalled when I stopped him mid flow to say that, even if as suggested this would be *"highly likely"* to regain *"total control"* of the situation; none of these procedures individually could be expected to improve my quality of life and taken together would create a level of impairment that would make me a life-long invalid. Whoops! To say he was unprepared for this is an understatement on a par with suggesting that Mary Berry has a bit of a knack for baking!!

Despite reeling from the brusqueness and inflexibility of the delivery, R and I fortunately had the common sense to go home and immediately produce a "cost-benefit" analysis. All the costs listed in black felt tip, benefits in red. We came up with 1 red: *"factoring in my age and general good health, potentially a 50% likelihood of successfully controlling symptoms for the next 5 years"*. Ironically we'd found these stats ourselves by trawling reputable health websites. We then endured a weekend of nightmares (literally) as we processed the implications, until I thought to write a "never to be sent" letter to the consultant.

Although it may be overly simplistic, I'm a great believer in "depression is anger taken inwards" and could feel from the sick feeling in my stomach that I had to do something to break the sense of darkness engulfing me. I was also desperate to identify why such profound fear had been generated by a mere 30 minute consultation. To be effective however the base line is that the writing MUST be uncensored, in order to side step the effort needed in keeping the lid on the something that feels immensely dangerous lurking in the shadows beyond the reach of my conscious mind. So I'm actually liberated by taking this first step alone with my pen and paper, until I've had chance to "name" the otherwise hard to acknowledge "negative" emotions.

Draft 1 "Never-to-be-sent letter"

Oi, you! Arrogant bastard. What in hell's name gives you the f-ing right to:

1. withhold and misrepresent information?

- yes, it has since transpired that you did know more from the CT scan than you were prepared to divulge

- yes, despite your assertions to the contrary, there are indeed other patients who have refused to go the chemo/ radiotherapy route

2. threaten me? - with quote: "a long and painful death" involving rank smells as my skin ulcerates! Simply because I had the temerity to refuse the equivalent of providing a blank cheque for you to surgically remove as much as you deemed appropriate once I was under the anaesthetic

Since you're the so-called "specialist" how come it's me who had to persist in the face of your "nothing's definite" stalling, to actually identify that in fact a potential 12 month decline with cancer is pretty much matched for the same time period by the horrors that I'll experience as a result of your recommendation of radical surgery followed by chemo + radiotherapy?

FYI: stats that WE had to uncover for ourselves show that of 12,000 women who undertook a similar course of treatment in the last year that data is available: 3,600 died within the year and, of the remainder, another 1/3rd within the next 5 years. So congratulations for a job well done: if you're "successful" even on your own terms, your suggested approach only controls the cancer in not quite half of the total sample. And at what cost? The 5,000+ "survivors" pay an extraordinary price, experiencing seriously debilitating symptoms such as lymphodoema, with the constant battle with pain to maintain mobility and to avoid serious infections. Not to mention the physical scarring that can wreck any hope of a sex life, along with emotional problems related to the invasiveness of treatment and residual trauma.

This is not life as I know it!

It may come as a surprise if you surround yourself with "Dr knows best" types, but you're not God – you can no more see the future than I can. And here's something to blow your mind, I probably know more than you do about where my body's up to: I've lived with the "stage 2 – precancerous cells" diagnosis for the last 20 years and I've been watching this latest development unfold over the last 8 months. You haven't even *taken* a full medical history – you're so totally focussed on task that I suspect my head could drop off and you wouldn't notice – or deem it relevant!

Do you even have the imagination to consider the living hell that is involved in your definition of "cure", or have you wilfully inured yourself to the double speak? If so, let me say it straight: there is nothing "therapeutic" about:

* "radiotherapy" – it produces "a radiation sickness syndrome of malaise, fatigue, nausea, anorexia and vomiting. This usually lasts for several months starting either during treatment or just after. It typically recurs with relatively normal periods in between" – but hey, that's OK, just delay making any plans because the relapses are so unpredictable. It's easy enough to put family life on hold for the duration ... NOT!

* chemotherapy is routinely used in about 50% of people with cancer "although it has been found to be of use in about 5% of cases". Plus, you have to love the irony, "chemotherapy agents are also carcinogenic and so cancer may develop after their use".

It's exactly the same strategy adopted in war zones to appease our collective consciences – use euphemisms like "collateral damage" and the fact that more civilians than service personnel are regularly killed during air strikes, magically disappears. Except with healthcare matters, the intention is meant to be benevolent. So isn't it 100 times worse that in behaving the way you did, you felt confident / justified in exploiting the power imbalance in our relationship, implying that I should tolerate so-called "side effects" or I'd effectively be choosing to commit suicide. You f-ing bastard – were you hoping that my husband wouldn't spot this blatant piece of emotional blackmail and collude with you to pressure flaky me into cooperating?

WRONG. You just gave us both nightmares trying to work out a way to retrieve the situation and get the level of compassionate care we deserve.

It's my body, my right to choose! So back right off with your state sanctioned FGM. You're made from the same mould as Nazi war criminals and I hope you rot in hell!!

PHEW ... better out than in! I'm not proud of this rant, but the concluding remarks "name" the specific fear and explain why it had such a profound effect. Since the tumour is located in my groin I'd clearly perceived the proposed procedures as both physical and emotional violation; then translated the resulting terror into a projection onto the consultant as abuser.

I'm guessing the clash of male and female energies was heightened by the consultant's manner; whilst he in turn, finding himself in the unfamiliar position of being "challenged", unwittingly acted to confirm the projection.

My understanding of psychoanalytic processes is limited, but this feels right – beneath the thinnest of veneers that we were taking part in a civilised exchange, we were effectively lobbing psychic lightning bolts at each other! It's hardly surprising that my initial sense of being battered proceeded to develop into a full scale panic attack, complete with shaking, dizziness and walking round in circles; once the week's events finally caught up with me.

Although recognising this at a head level is undoubtedly helpful, the real healing comes from the emotional release that was achieved through writing the letter. It is also consistent what Mary Lou Leavitt sees as the first skill of conflict resolution:

> This ability to name what seems to be going on, is crucial to getting the conflict out into the open, where we can begin to understand and try to deal with it. Such a skill is dangerous. It can feel – indeed it can be – confrontational.

Exactly as proponents of non-violent communication such as Archbishop Desmond Tutu explain, the first step to reconciliation is to express our pain in full. If all emotions are energy, then safely discharging the so-called negative ones unlocks the paralysis that comes from blocking them out of awareness, freeing the more compassionate ones to come to the fore.

In this case making me capable of a far more empathic second draft ...

Draft 2 "Never-to –be-sent" letter

Patient code .....   Appt date: x.y.z

Dear Mr A,

I am writing in the hope of clarifying some issues after my appointment with you last week and to start by saying that I now realise that with the packed schedule of patients that you see in clinic, I must have seemed like your worst nightmare.

You also weren't to know for instance that:

- both my parents died from cancer so, paradoxically, I don't fear it. I'm well aware that there are a vast number of cancers: some where you'd die of old age before they have an impact; others that are sufficiently localised like my Dad's bowel cancer, for him to live for another 20 years after his colostomy

- I actually developed lymphodoema after breaking my ankle, so know at first hand that if you were to remove the lymph nodes in my groin that I'd be living with excruciating pain for the rest of my life. Think toes so

swollen they're virtually fused together, making it a challenge to use even the thinnest wet wipe to clean between them. Plus legs that look and feel like sausages about to burst in the frying pan.

- I'm an "information is power" person and perfectly capable of understanding that every case you see involves a complex interplay of variables. Meaning that no 2 are the same therefore you work with "likelihoods" ie "if we x, then in y% of cases we'd expect z". So this was what we were geared for when we arrived for our appointment.

- My husband is dealing with his own living nightmare by using the extra hours at his disposal as a result of his early morning waking, to trawl (credible) web sites – hoping for "magic bullets" but settling for any stats he can find to help him understand what may lie ahead.

For all these reasons, reinforced by the fact that we were referencing the Macmillan booklet, so we'd clearly done our homework; you could have trusted that I had the capacity to take part in a comprehensive discussion of options. Given that you'd also been made aware I'd only been able to come to see you after receiving trauma counselling, due to my history of being so severely distressed by contact over the years with not 1, not 2, but 3! Gynaecologists; it seemed reasonable to expect a sensitive exchange.

Sadly, instead I found your approach inflexible and your manner brusque. In particular, whilst I agree entirely that it was your professional duty to inform me of the consequences of not proceeding with the treatment plan you were suggesting; I suspect the harshness of the words you chose to use reflected many emotions and dynamics of which you were barely conscious. Whatever forces were at play, the outcome was that both my husband and I suffered a weekend of nightmares and early morning waking as we replayed the exchange.

I do however know enough from features in the local paper that ward closures and bed blocking mean that you've almost definitely experienced the frustration of cancelled surgery. Set this against a background of cut backs to services and I totally "get" that the only way you can survive the demands of this type of work is by staying focussed on the task, genuinely believing that "doing something is better than doing nothing". It therefore makes absolute sense to me that given the length of time you've devoted to your training and the years subsequently invested in building up a vast body of skills and experience; that it would seem outrageous to you for me to choose what to you seems like certain death, over any level of hope that the procedures at your disposal could offer me.

What I'm struggling with however is the maxim: "just because we can, doesn't mean we should!" I've done a lot of research into pain management for instance and know that reliance on conventional pain meds can be reduced significantly if not totally eradicated by many more natural means (adequate sleep, balanced diet, gentle exercise, relaxation techniques, essential oils etc). So I know that whatever lies ahead, I will cope better if I can take a more holistic approach.

I'm assuming that you'd agree that I certainly have to better off if my system isn't having to contend with the unwanted effects of medication + various highly invasive procedures. And that my emotional well-being will benefit if I can watch the blue tits at the feeder outside the lounge window, pootle around trying to stay ahead in our organic veg patch and then sleep with a snoring dog on my bed. Such simple things, but SO life-affirming! Knowing myself as I do, the appearance of having any real choice in the matter is entirely an illusion: hospital routines, a parade of different staff and several months of major incapacity would crush my soul. So much so I fear there's every chance I'd simply give up the will to live.

I'm not writing this to ask for your understanding, because I think our positions are so far apart that we'll have to agree to differ. What I would hope is that by reminding you of the power imbalance in the doctor-patient role in general and the appalling risk of anything you do as a male gynaecologist and surgeon being perceived as a violation by your female patients; you will be infinitely more respectful towards others in the future. Or if, as may well be the case, because those who excel at task completion don't necessarily possess or value the "soft-skills" such as empathy; you find ways to better share this aspect of your role with colleagues in the multidisciplinary team.

Yours sincerely ...

This second draft is clearly much closer to something that could be shared to encourage a productive dialogue. I needed to reach the place where I could truly see that the intention wasn't to damage me, but I wouldn't be able to do this as long as I experienced Mr A's behaviour as a personal attack.

Taking into account that I'd been gearing up for the appointment since learning its date, I'd actually been managing a heightened level of anxiety for a fortnight beforehand. So the 30 minute contact time was only the tip of the ice berg, made infinitely worse by being taken completely by surprise by what came across as nothing better than a sales pitch. It's hardly surprising that at an emotional level I felt as if I'd stepped into the path of a 10 ton juggernaut, speeding down an unlit stretch of motorway, with just a pocket torch to warn the driver of my presence. But this analogy also meant that I could recognise that he in turn was equally unprepared and therefore just as shocked.

When I connected with my own humanity it was blindingly obvious that I was judging him on the basis of an episode that was entirely lacking context: that he too could have been having a bad day – stroppy teens at home, traffic hold ups on the way into work, chasing paperwork and the prospect of no breaks in a long and emotionally battering day.

To reiterate: *It's a question of finding ways to let go of our commitment to opposition and separation, to letting ourselves be open to our connectedness as human beings.*

I'm only too aware therefore that at one level it seems extremely un-Quakerly to "let rip" as I did, but my sense is that it's only after the hurts and fears have been safely expressed that there is room for compassion to come to the fore. I did however learn from the process involved in completing the exercise that what amounts to "forgiveness" of the person does not mean that I have to accept the behaviour. Nor was there a need for me to apologise in turn to achieve "closure". In fact the reverse was true and the process of writing helped me feel that my reactions were valid - I deserved better!

And it's this realisation of self-worth that untangled the final threads of hurt, because my calm inner voice showed me that rather than being punitive and engaging in further unproductive contact via complaints procedures, I could conserve my energy for life affirming experiences. This was so revitalising that for the first time in several months I was able to get out and walk our dog in the sunshine.

Of course, life isn't text book neat and I have a whole raft of prejudices that fuel my personal distrust of the medical model and will continue to make me cautious in any encounter with healthcare workers. I recently read for instance the account of the death of Charles II after he became ill with a kidney complaint

> "a series of physicians proceeded to bleed him, use cupping glasses and scarification, administer purgatives, blister the skin of his shaven head with red-hot cautery. For 4 days and nights he was "treated" by 14 physicians. At the end of this time he apologised for "an unconscionable time a-dying".

It makes me wonder if future generations will look back on current cancer treatments with the same level of incredulity? Already there is research that demonstrates that although consultants generally advise patients with prostate cancer to undergo surgery, despite a significant risk of post-operative erectile dysfunction along with a raft of other debilitating symptoms due directly to the procedures involved before and after treatment; many would not, in similar circumstances, follow their own recommendations. I certainly hope that soon society in general will become more alert to the irony that the same multi-national pharmaceutical companies that are supplying the meds used to treat our "cancer epidemic" are invariably the ones producing the pollutants, pesticides and food additives that may have triggered it!

*   *   *   *

Practicalities – the "F" word

Pray to Allah, but always tie up your camel!

It's strange to learn how many small deaths occur as R and I adjust to the diagnosis of a "life limiting condition" ("terminal illness" no longer the mot de jour), especially since without exception these nails in the coffin are intended to be supportive:

- meeting the (fabulous!) palliative care nurse who was the first person to listen to **my** story and then offer practical strategies for resolving issues we'd assumed simply needed to be endured

- ditto the home visit(!) of our GP to complete an advance treatment plan and DNR (Do Not Resuscitate), to restrict the "heroic measures" that might otherwise be applied, particularly by out of hours medics

- the arrival of the recliner chair that acts as a day bed to prevent me adding low back pain to my symptoms as a result of lying awkwardly on our settee – but takes eons before finally ejecting me (manufacturers in collusion with *Tena Lady*?) leaving visitors and various delivery personnel stranded on the doorstep and our dog with permanently crossed legs

- completing a will in order to gift treasures to specific family and friends, then ambushing 2 friends to witness it

- receiving notification that a weekly allowance will be paid to ease any financial pressures – thankfully in our case mainly funding a protracted programme of wining and dining those brave enough to visit, so invaluable for morale

But here's a thought: what happens if this transition period brings unlooked for benefits, rather than the doom and gloom that we're now socially conditioned to associate with dying? After all, what could be more empowering than gently and over time, having the chance to double check previously held views about the ceremonial aspects of death now we're faced with the imminent reality of booking a funeral service?

If R had been found himself having to deal with a police officer on the doorstep bearing the news that I'd wrapped our car around a tree, there's no way he'd have had the capacity to do other than line the pockets of the funeral industry by buying into a standard package of hearse, flowers and all the lavishness required as a public display of grief. Macabre as it undoubtedly is, we now at least have the opportunity to plan an event that is consistent with our beliefs ("in the manner of Quakers" so minimal music, no hymns or prayers and predominantly silent worship) and values ie primarily a support for the bereaved, yet also a celebration of my life, plus respectful of the environmental impact.

We'd always said for instance that the uniformity of modern grave yards are closer to the pristine ranks of war graves, which fails to reflect the quirkiness, let alone social history of church yards that, like the one in our own village dates back to Norman times. We're also freed up by the sense that deceased family members are around for us to chat to, as and when, rather than confined to their home neighbourhood 500 or so miles away.

Cremation therefore seemed like the best way of not taking up space unnecessarily after the event – with a big *BUT*: settings and services we've encountered have been dour! The use of fossil fuels to destroy the body and issue of toxic emissions also need to be factored in: with mercury from amalgam tooth fillings; dioxins from the plastics in and on conventional coffins; along with carbon monoxide, furans and other carcinogenic compounds being released into the atmosphere.

"Leave the land for the living" was the catchy cremationsists' *propaganda slogan in the mid twentieth century* but, as it says in the Natural Death Handbook ...*cremation does not provide any form of recycling, unless you agree that the recycling of mercury from tooth fillings entering the food chain via fall-out into the sea qualifies as such!*

5th edition p.153

Fortunately for us, this opportunity to reach an informed decision well in advance of the event actually means that we've had ample time to do the research and to discover that a woodland burial will tick all the boxes. Not least because we have a site on the edge of our village that R will drive past on most days, or have somewhere to sit and chat if he feels the urge. To then learn that the ground is owned by a long-established, family-run, independent funeral director, committed to facilitating whatever type of service we require; is an unlooked for advantage. Pure serendipity!!

No grave to be tended by our non-existent descendants and, as for the sticking point about taking up space - apparently it's an urban myth that if the entire half million people who die in Britain each year were to be buried, the whole country would be covered in cemeteries. In fact it would take 2,000 years to use the same acreage of land that farmers currently devote to set-aside. If these were all woodland burials, just imagine the fabulous wild-life corridors we'd be creating, as well as much needed oases of calm for their human counterparts.

So the plan is (weather permitting) to host an al fresco lunchtime party as a thank you to everyone who has done so much to support us through everything; during which friends can pick foliage and flowers from our garden to thread through my willow coffin as they say their "good byes". A Meeting for Worship held either in our home or in the memorial garden, completed by a short burial service. Funerals are for the living, so it feels wrong for me to try to be more prescriptive.

* * * *

Lessons in Etiquette

It's all so surreal! I have no idea how much my lack of energy is due to the hidden impact of this constant state of trying to plan ahead, so that in the not too distant future we'll be freed to get on with our lives for the remainder of time available. There is however certainly lots of scope for gallows humour when recounting for instance the uncharacteristic ease with which the authorities processed my "payment to die/death grant" and the irony that I'm now in receipt of the equivalent of the state pension that the Government were planning to deny me for another 7 years.

This only serves to highlight a whole raft of problems that arises associated with "etiquette", since I'm constantly reminded that people would prefer it if I'd take my dying with some seriousness:

Miss Manners Guide to Dying

- how to reply to casual enquiries about well-being from good friends who we nevertheless probably only bump into a few times a year? We've decided that M&S or the garden centre aren't the places to reply with "well actually ..."

- how to let family and friends know without leaving it so late they're wondering why our Christmas cards are only signed by R? Surprisingly, "sad news" headers on emails have generally been better received than phone calls. It gives all concerned chance to process the implications before replying; as well as allowing us to adapt a standard format to each person, rather than facing the challenge of starting from scratch and being battered by having to repeat the salient details with each one.

- how to convey the uncertainty of the prognosis, particularly because it's hopefully going to be a chance infection rather than the slow decline threatened by the consultant? And would I rather people remember me while I'm still able to garden, prepare meals and match them glass for glass, confident that the deterrent of liver cirrhosis is no longer a factor?!

- how to be good hosts whilst recognising that visitors may actually prefer to incur the extra cost involved in B&B for the "time out" that travelling to and fro provides?

- how to acknowledge the herd of elephants in the room when friends call in? (Just name it). And then how to gauge what is "too much detail"? Some people welcome facts to help them process implications; whereas with others even an apparently innocuous remark triggers memories or fears (change of facial colour or slipping to the floor in a dead faint would be real give-aways!)

- better to embrace the risk of "foot-in-mouth" syndrome than to walk on egg shells. The ribald laughter produced by gallows humour is the best medicine for me – I translate it as your willingness to be truly alongside us, salute your bravery and know therefore that should a remark go amiss, it'll be fixable

- how to politely fend off expressions of concern? Because there comes a point when I'm bored witless by all the dying palaver and am desperate to hear about holidays taken or planned, family skirmishes and all the day to day minutiae

- how much can be safely fitted into one day without "paying the price" and having to cancel a long-planned treat, thereby confirming the dreaded "invalid" role?

- how to avoid been seen as insensitive due to: the euphoria generated by the spiritual insights that are constantly unfolding; or that I'm gloating at my imminent release? *Mummy, mummy, why is gran-ma reading the Bible? Hush dear, she's swotting for her finals!* seems a propos.

- how to be alert to the enormity of what life is going to be for those remaining? I'm learning not to underestimate the power of Love, especially when words fail; particularly the healing potential in the Quaker tradition of "holding in the Light" friends who are distressed, or problems that seem insurmountable

It was only when I was forwarding this to a friend who was honest enough to admit to being desperate for some guidance about "how to be" around us, that I realised how closely the format matches Quaker's *Advices and Queries.* The WOW factor of this booklet comes from its format because it avoids laying down the law and simply prompts each reader to consider to what degree we are living true to our values (represented by the overlapping testimonies to Simplicity, Truth, Equality, Peace and, most recently, Sustainability). So it feels somehow fitting that my list isn't a prescriptive set of do's and don'ts, to allow room for ever shifting goal posts.

In turn another friend / ex colleague has kindly given me permission to share the following jokey questionnaire which she sent, in keeping with true social work tradition, which allows me to choose from and therefore accept graciously, without fear of appearing selfish all or any of her "services".

Supportive Friend Preferences Form Reference CB/JB

Please indicate preferences accordingly (circle/delete as appropriate)

Communication

1. **Letters:** yes   /   no

a) content: chatty / serious / humorous / encouraging / reflective

b) frequency: weekly / fortnightly / monthly / ad hoc

2. **Cards:** yes   /   no

type: natural beauty / humour / spiritual / selection

3. **Emails:** yes   /   no

4. **Phone calls:** yes   /   no

a) content: chatty / serious / listening to you

b) initiated by: self / initiated by supportive friend / either

5. **Texts:** yes   /   no

6. Gifts: yes / no (limited by postal restrictions!)

7. Prayer support: compulsory as this underpins all of the above and hopefully keeps the supportive friend 'on track'!

8. Other: yes / no (if yes, please specify)

Please note: preferences can be amended at any time.

Love from the supportive (I hope) friend, JB xx

Throughout all this I have been guilty of the most appalling insensitivities – being more anti-hero than hero in the unfolding drama:

- whatever made me quote Romeo's "parting is such sweet sorrow" for instance as friends were taking their leave? (A misplaced desire to acknowledge that we might be saying a permanent "goodbyes"?)

- or to offer to play surrogate ancestor from "the beyond" for a friend's son who was in dire need?

There is also an inevitability about being floored by the unexpected and feeling unable to communicate directly being stopped by fear it may be too hurtful. Or thinking the person may be too emotionally frail to cope, or even having direct communication which simply is not heard. Take for example an occasion we were visited by an 'old' friend who simply does not 'get' emotion and is unaware of her impact on others. She arrived on the doorstep wanting to stay for a few days to 'help out'.
Unfortunately, the helping out was at a cost as she didn't want to drive, or walk the dog or help around the house and was not influenced by direct communication – "x this is not working". The amount of frustration left behind required another "never to be sent" letter.

Unsent Letter to my friend Who Doesn't "Get" Emotions and is not self-aware

I'm an idiot! What possessed me to think that after not meeting for years, your refused invitations and token email exchanges for birthdays and Christmases; that we could rebuild bridges now that I'm dying? I'm so profoundly shocked by the way you left this morning – with no acknowledgement of the effort we've invested over the last week in trying to make your stay as pleasurable or least distressing as possible.

It's all about mixed messages: you said that you'd come to help out, but … don't want to drive, so can only accompany R on shopping trips that he could have completed in a fraction of the time. You're not used to dogs, so didn't feel comfortable taking turns walking ours. All your efforts simply tripled the demands on us; requiring us to run (or, in my case, hobble) around providing materials and tools, then making good the work you said you knew how to do. Ditto having to be asked to help carry out plates and glasses for the BBQs arranged especially for you.

My energy levels swing erratically between plus and minus 30% but until you're faced with the reality of juggling priorities like showering, getting dressed, making a drink to wash down the painkillers; it's impossible to appreciate how much my world has had to shrink and how much I hate the resulting dependence on others. Hence my responsibility for pacing myself, so that at least those around me are not dealing with a sodden mess of misery because I've overdone it yet again and am wiped out!

It was therefore a double whammy, really rubbing salt into my wounds, to be forced to deplete this finite resource by both having to explain, then remedy the very jobs I had until recently been able to complete, so effortlessly and unaided. With hindsight it was a salutary experience to have other friends over for lunch whilst you were here, to watch how they apparently effortlessly anticipated and responded to needs: refilling glasses, telling R to sit down whilst they fetched whatever ... and done with such joy. So it's not that we had unrealistic expectations.

Not the most patient of people until now, I'm learning that biting my tongue goes with the territory when fending off poorly thought through expressions of sympathy. Yet you were able to take me totally by surprise by asking outright for two items you liked! Didn't it make you the slightest bit uncomfortable to be effectively grave robbing at this time?

I find it more astounding however that you're actually the only one of our visitors who hasn't been able to join the dots when it comes to appreciating the body-blow represented by my need, a week earlier, to move my bedroom downstairs. What however was most distressing, was to have my attempts to apologise for being a bit under par by describing the roller coaster of emotions associated with the never-ending losses that frequently come close to overwhelming me; met with what I now recognise as your trade mark impassive "Right".

It's as if you should have a display unit on your forehead that lights up whenever emotion is shown, with the phrase "does not compute". Even though I can now appreciate that your silence may be more bemused rather than necessarily critical, it is nevertheless just as hurtful as your previous knee-jerk retorts that made me out to be the problem because I was "too sensitive".

Unlike other friends, you've never volunteered your own take on my situation, not even its impact on you. In fact you don't volunteer anything, let alone "thank you", so any and all our efforts disappear into a resoundingly silent black hole. Instead it's been literally breath-taking to follow your non-sequiturs, when you segue around the minefield of emotional content, back to safe ground such as anecdotes about your family. We laugh at the gaucheness of Sheldon Cooper, the science nerd in 'The Big Bang Theory'; conveniently minimising the very real distress his lack of social skills create for those in his fall out zone. So perhaps not surprisingly I was left asking myself "who's the adult here?"; facing the reality that despite the fact I have only a few more months left to look forward to, it will always be me / us accommodating you.

The gift that you've given me however is finally to understand why we could not and will never become the "good friends" I've yearned to be. Your visit has shown how your life is measured in a series of equations: so that on your terms you paid to travel to see us therefore we owed you the food and drink we provided for your stay. We would (of course!) have declined any offers to buy us a take away or wine as thanks for our hospitality; but it's so sad to realise that you have no idea that such social interchanges leave everyone feeling good.

I'm therefore guessing (but feel safe that I'm correct in assuming), that you've taken time away from your family because "that's what friends do when one of them is dying". At this point however I need quality not quantity, kindred spirits not visitors driven by "musts", "oughts" and "shoulds". Instead, we've been left as if picking up the pieces after being hit by a force of nature that is totally impervious to the trail of devastation left in its wake.

So, thank you from the bottom of my heart for provoking the crisis that validates my guilt-ridden decision to prioritise my own needs and in due course somehow find the words to put off any future visits from you. It's highlighted our appreciation that "Life's too short" to just go through the motions. But most of all, I will be eternally grateful for you showing me, albeit inadvertently, that just because we're so different, doesn't make me wrong.

Your friend Chris xx

By writing the letter, it became possible to capture the previously free-floating speech bubbles of conversations I wish I'd had whilst my friend was here and in so doing, ensure that the attendant emotions would be safely contained. Better still it allowed old hurts to surface and be healed - a profound lesson in uncovering the innate wisdom in the over-used but under-examined commandment *"to love thy neighbour as thyself"*. With step one being the need to start by loving myself!

What resulted was the mind-blowing realisation that without this I'd never achieve the compassion to ever accept others "warts and all". If I continued to buy into what were, after all, only the criticisms I inferred from her behaviour, I'd be condemned to perpetuate the cycle of mutual blaming. Since fundamentally the sole person we can change is ourselves, I also needed to stop feeling that it is my friend's responsibility to fix her very real discomfort by pulling some rabbit out of the hat. Like peeling layers of an onion, this made way for the realisation that we're both doing the best we can in impossible circumstances.

Magically I'm now able to "listen behind her words": rather than focussing on the negatives to be thankful for the laughter we'd shared when we regressed whilst playing board games and grateful for the things she did for us during her stay.

> *When words are strange or disturbing to you, try to sense where they come from and what has nourished the lives of others. Listen patiently and seek the truth which other people's opinions may contain for you. Avoid hurtful criticism and provocative language. Do not*

allow the strengths of your convictions into making
statements or allegations that are unfair or untrue.
Think it possible that you may be mistaken.

(Advices & Queries #17)

It is no exaggeration to say that I have received an unlooked for gift in learning that it is possible to care for someone, whilst simultaneously protecting myself from the jangling dynamics that are inevitable when two people operate from such diametrically opposed positions. It was therefore pure serendipity that she "missed" my request that she leave early, because not clued in to social nuances she misunderstood my distress as an expression of concern for her well-being.

So, though it was a close call, I only realised that we have indeed rebuilt bridges after I was able to take into account the strong preconceptions I'd held about the form these should take. I'd anticipated a fairy tale, happy ever after ending of, if not identical twins joined at the hip, at least kindred spirits – little realising that what I needed was to be able to honour our individual uniqueness.

Thank goodness the universe knows better than to bow to what we think we want, but provides us instead with what we actually need!

Dream sequence

Back in the cavern, is the boat getting bigger or am I shrinking as I distil down to the basic essence of what it is to be me? I seem to be in several places at once: cocooned in the feathered cloak in the bottom of the boat, whilst simultaneously an onlooker, floating above and slightly to one side. Though hard to compute, there's also a new self, slipping out of the physical body to emerge like the DNA coding of a Viking ancestor. I like this new me: she's vibrant, unapologetic about her vitality, not only capable of standing her ground but expecting respect for honouring her femaleness. I sit at the back of the boat alongside the shaman and continue to consolidate and play with this unfamiliar energy.

At some point it becomes apparent that we're being drawn towards the shore and touching land after so long sends all my senses into overload. It's as if nothing has ever been so clearly defined before: the simple act of walking up the beach a celebration of coordination at the feel and sound of my feet alternately sinking and extricating themselves from the sand. I'm thrilled by the swing of my hips and shoulders as I brace to crest the dunes to take stock of our surroundings. Meantime the shaman has laid my still- cocooned-self tenderly by a fire and is intent on preparing something in the pot hanging over its flames.

Sitting silently amongst the roots of a tree I'm astounded to see a pack of wolves abandoning their camouflage and willing to carry on their everyday lives despite my presence. I have no

idea how much time elapses as I watch, entranced. My senses,
already on overload, achieve a level of euphoria that leaves me
almost uncomfortably lightheaded. As if in recognition, an
older, silvery coated female detaches from the group and
comes directly to me. I kneel and lean towards her so that we
can touch foreheads.

And I start to cry. Howling, lung-bursting, heart-wrenching
grief that I had no idea I even had the capacity to carry.
Leaning further forward to lay my head against the earth, I
spread my arms wide but don't know if the embrace is to give
or receive comfort. It feels as if every wracking breath is an
apology for hurts caused by actions or omissions in this and all
my previous life times. I'm so mortified by the never-ending
stream of my many carelessness's, but mostly by my complicity
in the systematic plundering of Earth's resources; that it would
be a relief to simply stop breathing rather than have the
awareness of taking part in such wilful destruction.

The she-wolf makes no attempt to soothe me, but her dignity
as she provides silent witness gives me a growing sense that
there is a possibility that even such a violation can be endured,
if not forgiven. As dusk falls and she slips back to her pack, the
shaman comes to gather the shed tears and returning to the
fireside, wordlessly pours them into the cooking pot. Feeling all
my strength drain from me, I lie down alongside my cocooned
self and am engulfed by a welcome oblivion.

The next morning after packing up camp and as we're
preparing to return to the boat, the shaman reaches out to

pass me a handful of crystals, then steps behind me to tie them around my neck. Still subdued by the events of the previous day, I touch them and recognise them as the gift of tears – my throat aches and my eyes threaten to overflow yet again – but instead I am engulfed by a deep sense of peace. It is as if these jewels symbolise the vast, compassionate life force uniting the ground beneath our feet, the river that is taking us unerringly towards our destination and the overarching sky.

Chapter 3: The departure lounge

Context: stress management

Despite the hype extolling the excitement of travel, an equally inescapable aspect of it is the pure tedium of hanging around waiting for events to unfold that are mainly beyond our control. The gatekeeping medical processes that have got me to this point involve much the same frenetic bursts of activity as those in airports; similarly interspersed with interminable waiting, delays and even cancellations. The parallels with this phase of my dying are inescapable: in fact I may as well be embarking on a long-haul flight in economy class, because I am suddenly aware that I am surrounded by so many others heading to the same destination!

Just as travelling in real-time can be consumed by "sweating the small stuff", worrying about what lies ahead (is the hotel still a building site?) or what we're leaving behind (is the gas turned off? ... can friends be trusted to water the tomatoes?); it is SO hard for me to stay focussed on what truly matters in the present. But this has to be a priority now if I am to live each day to the full, in order to make the most of the time remaining. Reminded by a neighbour's observation "keeping busy then", another popular option I am faced with is to "kill time": doing whatever is the equivalent of mindlessly trawling through duty-free, bingeing in fast food outlets and employing Vulcan mind control techniques to elicit good news from any available staff.

What I am hoping for instead is that there is a way to use this interlude to achieve a better understanding of the dynamics that underpin what I am currently going through. Ideally this will re-awaken tried and tested coping mechanisms, so that despite the grim prognosis I can embark on a programme of damage limitation. This coincides however with what feels like an almost sinful admission: that for the first time since becoming an adult, I now have absolutely no demands made on my time or expectations made of me. I am at liberty to do whatsoever I wish!! With one proviso – challenging the 3 toed sloth for its title of world's sleepiest mammal, based on its need for 13 hours per day.

Until now, it never occurred to me that so much freedom would be gained as a result of being forced to delegate most of the "maintenance" tasks involved in daily living - especially since the instruction to 'avoid operating heavy machinery' conveniently resonates with my dislike of vacuuming! So, although abandoning the deeply engrained Protestant work ethic will, I am sure, throw up a great many challenges (not least the default guilt setting of being unable to prevent R working himself to a shadow to compensate); if all I have to do is learn how to allow myself to luxuriate in this freedom, I'm up for it! Happiness, after all, is said to be achieved by behaving in ways that combine both purpose and meaning – a tough job, but someone's got to do it!

Although it is still early days, taking this route has already proved a revelation, because it turns out that far from exploring new territory I am effectively only re-familiarising myself with processes that I have navigated seamlessly in other contexts. The problem has been that the shock of the diagnosis was such a body blow that for several months I now realise I was robbed of the ability to think clearly. There is, after all, no getting away from it: **as soon as "Cancer" is mentioned, life as we know it ceases.** Even for those for whom it turns out to be a scare and all is in fact well, the time spent waiting for results has to act as a wake-up call to what it means to be mortal.

As with all problem-solving however, success involves being absolutely focussed on addressing the core issue, rather than being distracted by peripheral details. It is therefore not actually about the early morning waking, the pain, tiredness, whatever ... these are (just?) the symptoms. Chasing these may well achieve significant respite in the short-term, but unless the underlying cause is remedied I will always be playing catch up.

Yes. I know cancer is massive yet if we break it down into specifics, for me the base line is that I am dealing with stress – pure and simple!

Despite being loathe to add further to the shelves of literature already devoted to methods for retaining a sense of perspective whilst managing both change and stress; there are concepts that I have picked up in the course of my professional life that I suspect may be less familiar to others. They have the added bonus of providing shortcuts for analysing the uniqueness of our individual circumstances, on which foundations for a coherent action plan can be built for anticipating what may lie ahead.

To begin therefore I have provided brief summaries of four such issues and then, because they overlap to a significant degree, in the remainder of the chapter I have woven them together with illustrations from my own experiences, to explore what may be implications of wider relevance.

*   *   *   *

The creative potential of change

Although life repeatedly demonstrates that "the only constant is change", it is a major achievement if we can live peaceably with the level of uncertainty that this produces. Hence the humility of Reinhold Niebur's appeal on behalf of troops about to embark into battle during World war II, that has become known as *the Serenity prayer*

God give us the grace
to accept with serenity the things we cannot change,
courage to change the things that should be changed,
and wisdom to know the difference

Nevertheless, the base line remains – we thrive when we experience security and stability. So by its very nature, change is potentially threatening. But in the same way that stress is more complex and encompasses being under too little, as well as too much pressure; so change is multi-faceted and can also be a gift, inextricably tied to both our personal growth and evolution as a species.

Just as Buddhists remind us that the bucket of water drawn from the river is not the river; I have a growing realisation that the concept of change is restricted unnecessarily if it is defined simply as the act of making choices between plan A or, plan B. Having had more time to consider its subtler nuances I am coming to the conclusion that, to be truly open to the opportunities change makes available to us, we need to appreciate its fluidity and trust that it reflects matters beyond those that we can readily discern. As a Quaker friend recently commented, a helpful rule of thumb when it comes to recognising when "*Way opens*" as part of the big picture rather than our own small-scale wish-fulfilment, is because it is too painful to ignore the promptings and not act - even though the consequences of our action will inevitably take us way out of our comfort zone!

It helps to remember too that whether we resist or harness it, change is a process. Like moving house for instance, it is neither a single event under which a line can be drawn when it has been completed, nor a linear unfolding of related activities. In fact, the more I start to trust that being in the flow is actually in my best interests (and certainly less energy sapping than trying to swim against the tide), so it seems to reveal that at its heart change shares the same intangible features as all mystical experiences. It offers us the greatest gift - nothing less than the means by which we can discern our life's purpose.

Sometimes we need to take the lead in making change happen especially when events may be impacting on us. The following is a tool which I make use of.

i. The Change equation (Beckhard. Harris 1987)

Whether the changes we are facing are forced on us by external circumstances or chosen deliberately, there are certain factors that are amenable to our input, as shown in the following formula:

$$C \int D K V > Cost$$

This translates as;- positive Change is a ∫unction of Discomfort (with the current situation); Knowledge both of how we got into this mess so we don't repeat the same mistakes, as well as what may be done to resolve it; plus the Vision of what specifically this change would look like. These must be worth more than (>) the potential Cost either psychological and/or financial cost involved.

Example:

Change is required because my partner is constantly crying. Partner has always perceived self as 'strong' and crying as weakness.

My level of **Discomfort** = High – I become distressed at his/her distress.

Knowledge – we initially said we wouldn't cry in front of each other and he/she said he/she would be strong for me.

What can I do if anything? Let him/her know that I know of the crying. Acknowledge that crying is a strength especially in these circumstances as it helps as a safety valve. Suggest a change to the rules and we cry together. Suggest counselling. Suggest he/she uses the shed as his/her crying place. Do nothing?

Vision – He/she begins to identify that crying is a positive expression of emotion as well as an expression of concern.

Cost – She/he may lose face/get angry/become more distressed. She/he may leave (low possibility).

So the question now is, is the value in doing something about it greater than the value in not doing anything? If the answer is yes – take action.

I use this as a map to ensure that each aspect has been sufficiently explored to provide me with a coherent plan of action - although sometimes not until the sense of being "caught between a rock and a hard place" forcibly reminds me that something has been overlooked that is creating and impasse rather than allowing me to move forward! If this happens however the clues are unavoidable because, in keeping with the mind-body link, stagnation can occur at any or every level. There may well be physical symptoms such as the digestive irregularity associated with Irritable Bowel Syndrome; mental lethargy; emotional distress and spiritual dislocation.

ii. The physiological effects of stress

Just as we ignore the flashing *check engine light* in our car at our peril, so this diagram illustrates what happens when we repeatedly over-ride the body's various warning signals that all is not well. By reacting to the symptom (increasing tiredness) rather than the cause (long term exposure to stress) we are relying on the false energy supplied by adrenaline to keep going. This creates a system wide knock on effect including a compromised immune system and therefore lowered resistance to disease; erratic spikes and troughs in blood sugar levels resulting in swings in both mood and energy levels; and hormonal imbalance affecting reproductive health, sleep disturbance, weight gain.

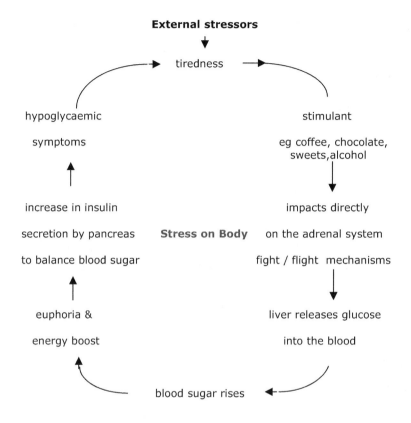

External stressors

tiredness

hypoglycaemic
symptoms

stimulant
eg coffee, chocolate,
sweets, alcohol

increase in insulin
secretion by pancreas
to balance blood sugar

Stress on Body

impacts directly
on the adrenal system
fight / flight mechanisms

euphoria &
energy boost

liver releases glucose
into the blood

blood sugar rises

It is the equivalent of trying to drive with a faulty accelerator pedal: sometimes flooring it produces only minimum response; other times, the slightest pressure causes such an over-reaction that it makes us fearful. A highly distressing aspect is that these waves of anxiety can surge over us at the very time we are actually sitting quietly. It is as if the very absence of a perceived threat sets alarm bells ringing: *"I must be missing something"*.

Bizarrely this can be taken as good news, because what it means is that a significant part of what we may be experiencing post-diagnosis is NOT necessarily caused by the growth of the tumour! Rather than a product of the dreaded cancer, it could instead be the logical result of counter-productive coping strategies, such as relying on sugar and caffeine highs to compensate for the loss of our "get up and go". This knowledge alone means it may be realistic to aim to deal successfully even with debilitating and dramatic symptoms such as anxiety and panic attacks produced by *impaired adrenal functioning*, without adding to the cocktail of medications already prescribed.

This is just one of a myriad of examples where "knowledge is power" because by accurately defining the problem, we are more likely to seek solutions in the appropriate places.

Abdominal breathing exercises, massage, visualisation and mindfulness may be low-tech and the boost provided by re-asserting control does not magically cancel out the dire aspects of our situation; but they come with a virtually cast iron guarantee that the resulting calm will improve our decision-making capacity and ability to "stop and smell the roses".

The implicit message, that despite everything we can still trust our capacity for self-care, is invaluable in terms of maintaining our resilience for dealing with whatever lies ahead.

iii. Perspective: use it or lose it!

In my experience the single most important concept when it comes to managing stress is the realisation that what we refer to as "**Stress" is** a function of our perception – **our reaction to events, NOT the events themselves.**

Which is simultaneously profoundly simple and yet extraordinarily hard to apply when we find ourselves up against it! The same experience, being made redundant for instance, can be seen as an opportunity (a spur to go freelance, retrain, travel); but if the mortgage payments or the ability to meet other basic needs will be jeopardised, it turns into a crisis.

Underlying all this is the notion of perspective, because if it is our attitude to these events that creates stress, then logically reductions in stress levels can only be achieved by a change in perception.

I am however only too aware however that it would be crassly insensitive to suggest that there is any upside to receiving the diagnosis of a degenerative disease. Just as I am personally irritated beyond endurance by the pseudo- mantras that state that positive thinking (with the implicit "done properly") is a cure all – they simply add guilt to the equation when we then infer that we've somehow wished bad things on ourselves!

Nevertheless, recognising that the issue of perspective stems from "the stories" that we tell ourselves and it is these that can be modified, is immensely liberating. Doing so also enables us to be more authentic and able to bear to live for the moment rather than the more typical responses of catastrophizing about the future or subsumed by regrets for missed opportunities in the past. This demonstrates a key point that IF (a significant proviso and by no means a "given") life's events have enabled us to become sufficiently resilient, we do have the capacity to achieve the psychological boost that results from taking control rather than feeling victimised by events.

iv. How to avoid 'making a drama out of a crisis'

As a social work student I was taught that all crises have the potential to be hugely positive because they not only force us to develop a new range of strategies for coping with the unfamiliar; but then, having survived these difficulties, they also contribute to increased resilience in preparation for future setbacks. At the same time however, the crucial importance of avoiding being caught up in the Victim – Rescuer – Persecutor "script" was drummed in to us.

It is after all arrogant beyond belief to assume that on the basis of limited contact, we as strangers could "fix" issues (and in so doing inadvertently "rescue" or implicitly "blame" those in need of assistance), that could well have been causing problems for literally generations. Instead, irrespective of the severity of the crisis, we generally saw families survive best when encouraged to draw on their own resources; with our role invariably to provide short-term, practical support.

Murphy's Law after all is that "Life Happens" to us all, but typically with such intensity and at a time when we are already so over-stretched, that we need a boost beyond our own resources.

I also repeatedly notice however that with even a brief respite from these pressures, we unwittingly shed outmoded coping strategies and an innate capacity is mobilised to develop responses more relevant to our current circumstances. An unlooked for bonus that paradoxically only such turmoil could have released.

All of which is consistent with concepts initially popularised in the mid-seventies by Eric Berne, founder of Transactional Analysis (TA). In books such as *The games people play* he illustrated that much of our behaviour is learned from our past exchanges, involving dynamics of which we are largely unaware. To get the best results from a given situation we therefore need to develop ways to check the relevance of this historical data and, if it is outmoded, to update it.

The simplest example is that when dealing with authority figures, we have to fight the tendency to regress to the passive or rebellious behaviours we learned in childhood when relating to our parents and others who had power over us.

If instead we can remind ourselves that we are adults, looking for a "win-win" solution, it is easier to avoid adopting stances that turn us into doormats, bullies or martyrs.

Looking around it is relatively easy to recognise those who operate from this "poor me" default setting, because they leave us feeling drained and manipulated. But the "pay-off" is seductive in its familiarity: if at an unconscious level one party believes that life has dealt them a rubbish hand, then there will be others who enjoy the sense of superiority that comes either from protecting or blaming them.

These "games" are commonplace wherever people interact, but assume a potentially more sinister element when institutionalised within organisations particularly when, as in any health setting "the stakes" are literally life or death.

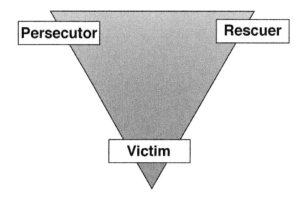

The Drama Triangle

(Stephan Karpman 1960's)

In terms of the western medical model for instance, the outmoded relationship of doctor as expert, patient as passive recipient of services, creates an unhelpful power imbalance; not least because playing the "doctor knows best" game requires that patients abdicate responsibility for their own health. Interestingly, as the diagram of the *drama triangle* above shows, this is just as uncomfortable for the doctors whose role switches to victim when faced with inadequate resources and driven by procedures designed to forestall litigation; rather than genuine concern with the quality of patient care.

What characterises "games" however is their "hidden agendas". These occur when, rather than an overt exchange between 2 or more individuals or groups that is mutually beneficial; one, if not both, are disadvantage by the outcome. Rather than coming from an "I'm OK – You're OK" stance that seeks a "win-win" solution, actions that are instead driven by motives that are largely unconscious can only involve manipulation and lead to a nagging sense of dissatisfaction.

The tragedy is that intentions and motives in healthcare settings are invariably benevolent, but circumstances conspire to trap all concerned in a series of classic "no-win" situations.

Information sharing for instance is a potential minefield: with medics required to gauge the sensitivity of data and selectively withhold facts based on what they believe to be in the patient's best interests; whilst in turn, patients can be actively discouraged from volunteering pertinent information sensing the practitioner's bias or other preoccupations.

Since most interactions in this setting are already emotionally laden there is also a huge potential for assumptions and prejudices to further undermine effective communication. This is compounded by traits commonly experienced amongst the general population, but which inevitably assume greater significance when caring for those with chronic health problems.

The tendency to confuse action with effectiveness for instance is familiar to all of us from times spent caught on a hamster wheel of working harder rather than smarter. But when it comes to palliative care, the assumption that it is better to be seen to be doing something - anything, rather than nothing, can have catastrophic results.

It is sadly commonplace for instance to hear patients in the last few weeks of life expressing regret about their decision to pursue medical interventions, having confused the doctor's intention to prolong rather than improve quality of life; when they realise with hindsight that what they needed to be concentrating on instead, was saying timely goodbyes.

There are however also "Informed Patient Programmes" designed for those experiencing chronic health problems where, as with palliative care teams, both service provider and user share the responsibility for being proactive in health care planning. Such Adult-Adult exchanges aim to dispel the notion for instance that some information is so potentially "damaging" that it needs to be withheld.

The benchmark for assessing the integrity of such services is that patients are assumed to have the mental capacity (unless proven otherwise) to make educated decisions and crucially, are supported emotionally and practically, to come to terms with the realisation that there are no real choices – just a series of least damaging alternatives. This for me is the true measure of *not making a drama out of a crisis.*

What all this teaches me ....

- "name, listen then let go" strategy for ensuring that I am addressing the central problem rather than the symptoms, allowing time to hear what my inner wisdom can contribute and not putting restrictions on potential solutions

- **70:30 rule** – stop while 30% of energy remains to repay energy overdraft. Changing pace throughout the day will allow me to recharge, get a sense of achievement and honour commitments

- use the "infinite why" exercise to check that my goals are truly what I desire and identify the most effective way of achieving them eg *I want to be rich – why – because I can spend less time in a job I hate,* actually suggests that finding ways of making the work more satisfying or looking for a different job, is likely to be more effective!

- use **SMART** (**S**pecific, **M**easurable, **A**chievable, **R**ealistic, **T**ime limited) details to support in visualising short, medium and long-term outcomes and as a reminder to break tasks into small but effective steps, to increase chances of successfully realising them

- build on positives – they say it takes 3 "good" experiences to outweigh 1 "bad" one, so the "gratitude" exercise is a useful way of refocussing and making the space for beauty and creativity to impact in my life

- Smile – better still, laugh! If a "friend" is the person who brings out the best in us, be my own best friend and look out for Life's "gifts"

- avoid unrealistic goals, particularly those that involve a sense of being "deprived" of favourites or "pressured" against my natural inclination and check these out periodically with a friend (coach / mentor) to increase the likelihood of staying on track

- remember the instructions for using oxygen masks in the event of the plane's cabin de-pressurising: put my own on first otherwise I won't be able to assist others. It is healthy to prioritise my own needs – *if I never say no, what is my "yes" worth?*

- build in a daily routine for meditation / prayer and rest free from interruption and practice mindfulness exercises in the midst of activities

- focus on activities that have purpose and meaning **for me** ie wildlife gardening connects me with nature, the seasons and my local community creating a joy that even cancer cannot dent

- **CELEBRATE successes!!**

Don't Quit

* * * *

Reality check

R and I now realise that the shock created by receiving bad news is a blessing in disguise, because it produced a numbness which helped us to continue to function on automatic pilot as we wove our way through the different stages of grieving. On one level it doesn't make the reality any less excruciating, but we were cushioned to a degree by knowing that if the stages of grieving can be so clearly charted, others have been here too - and survived!

So recognising the *denial* ("this is all a bad dream, they'll phone and apologise for a mix up in the test results"), *bargaining* ("if I start taking better care of myself ..."), *anger* ("why me? why now?"); means we can trust that although it currently seems desperately unlikely, ultimately we will become *reconciled* to the situation. Which, meantime gives us a better chance of making our remaining time together as positive as possible.

For the same reason I find checklists such as the one that follows disproportionately reassuring: useful for establishing a base line against which progress can be measured - or an indicator of when things are starting to unravel! I have included one here to help in "naming" the extent of potential problems, because rather than acting promptly as the first red flags are detected, I share with many others the tendency to under play the severity of distress; failing to appreciate the cumulative impact of each apparently small but significant issue.

High stress levels may show as:

- Feelings of powerlessness – trapped, no available choices
- Sense of being overwhelmed even by minor tasks
- Inability to concentrate, "fuzzy brain" and poor memory
- Extreme mood swings: uncharacteristic irritability/ flashes of anger
- Loss of confidence, indecisiveness +/or erratic decision making
- Sleeplessness / unrefreshing sleep or excessive sleeping
- Lack of energy and motivation, "tired all the time"
- Food cravings / comfort eating, increased reliance on stimulants eg coffee, then alcohol /cigarettes to unwind
- Problems within emotional relationships, loss of sex drive
- Tendency to brood / anticipate negative outcomes
- Hyperactivity, anxiety and panic attacks
- Depression, feelings of worthlessness / being out of control
- Physical symptoms eg migraines, high blood pressure, digestive upsets, low back pain; difficulty throwing off minor ailments
- Addictions, risk taking / self-harming behaviours
- Suicidal feelings +/or actions

Itemising the different elements is also a useful starting point to targeting those that we are in the position to change: dealing with memory fog by making lists on a chalk board in the kitchen so bits of paper don't get lost. Reaching for a few squares of quality chocolate, rather than mindlessly consuming whole packs of horribly processed instant fixes and adding nausea to the symptom list! It is certainly not a given that everyone receiving (or caring for someone with) a terminal diagnosis will develop the full range of symptoms; so it is a crucial reminder that if they become debilitating, counselling (and perhaps medication to buy time for the former to provide relief) would invariably be effective.

We are blessed to have an extremely empathic GP who listened as R recounted all but the last 2 symptoms and then provided a prescription for meds to address the anxiety attacks, because these were the most problematic. She pointed out however that they were not geared to helping him with the early morning waking, which came a close second and was contributing to his spiralling exhaustion.

The packet remains unopened because the most effective thing that she did was to listen, patiently and without judgement - and then confirm that everything he was experiencing was absolutely valid in the circumstances! Just knowing that the meds are there also provides a very real psychological safety net.

Applying the Change Equation

There have, of course, been times following the diagnosis that I too have indulged in fantasies of miracle cures, ranted against the universe or wasted time wondering about karmic retribution. This is what it means to be human and *Discomfort* simply isn't a big enough word for the level of pain and distress. But this is also the spur to make me seize every opportunity to take charge of the elements that are within my control and make sure that I do not waste air space on those that I cannot change.

In fact I am now convinced that greatest danger when faced with such life changing events is to **under**-react: I've heard so many people say *"well at least, hitting rock bottom means the only way is up"* – only to find that the unimaginable continues to be shovelled down! The stereotypical British stiff upper lip and the protective mechanism of numb denial make a potent combination, summarised by "don't make a fuss"; which ill prepares us for *"just when you'd've thought things couldn't get any worse – they did!!"*

As time has passed however it has definitely become easier to access and apply *Knowledge* from other contexts:

- adapting the Learning Cycle model that recognises that the phase of "*conscious incompetence*" is a necessary step in developing new skills (4 stages of competence model. Noel Burch)

This meant that I could factor in the inevitable sense of being overwhelmed by the enormity of the challenges we faced and rather than sinking under their combined weight, recognise them as yet another element within the general discomfort involved in adjusting to change

- Crisis Intervention theories that state that we have about 6 weeks before we develop coping mechanisms to enable us to adjust to even the most painful or disruptive shift in circumstances.

I regret how hard R and I still tend to drive ourselves, assuming that somehow the next rabbit we pull from the hat will provide the solution to what is in reality a series of "no wins".

It means that resources that are already seriously overstretched require ever more desperate measures to be sustained, until frequently brought to the brink. I find that I need to forcibly remind myself that chronic ill-health is amongst the top causes of job loss, relationship breakdown and spiralling financial problems. In keeping with the above however, the base line is that I have been able to hang on by repeating the simple statement: *this too will pass!*

Discovering therefore that just when we need our decision-making to be at its most effective, we were so far out of our depth that our knee-jerk responses were more likely to compound rather than retrieve earlier misjudgements. Yet somehow we resisted the very real desire to batten down the hatches by trying to go it alone.

Instead, when we could barely get ourselves dressed each day, we had friends who put their own lives on hold in order to for instance attend and record the information we were given during appointments. It is terrifying to have the experience of being stripped over-night of all semblance of professional competence, so "thank yous" fall far short! This note taking gave us a baseline that we could return to until we could bear to hear what we were being told and even months later gradually start to assimilate the ramifications.

In the early post-diagnosis days, 2 simple strategies repeatedly proved their worth. When we were feeling bull-dozed by threats of what the consultant termed a "fast-receding window of opportunity", we behaved counter-intuitively and insisted instead on *time to sleep on it.* Then, because inevitably sleep itself proved evasive, we used the time to make endless lists: analysing best and worst case scenarios and in doing so, freed up the energy required to explore specific practical resources to complement the "life skills" type of *Knowledge*.

Although we discovered that there is an essential paradox in needing to know enough to even formulate questions that will prove helpful, selective web searches have already proved invaluable in terms of managing my anxieties about what lies ahead. So yes, I am confident that I can continue to research the stats, ask those in the know (patients and medics) and then make an informed decision based on an assessment of the least damaging alternatives.

Then there is the deeper "gut" *Knowledge* that shores me up despite the prognosis: the fact is that there are always choices – even if it is only the decision to buy time to respond rather than react to events. It is this that counsels compassion, to not exhaust myself covering all bases but rather to leave space for circumstances to evolve in their own time. To trust ultimately that **Amor vincit omnia** *(Love conquers all)* and if/when the time comes that I am totally dependent on those around me, they too will find the resources to draw on this well spring of love.

In terms of obstacles that can de-rail even my best intentions, having recently retired any *Financial* problems are less of an issue than they would have been even 12 months ago. In turn, navigating the potential minefield of *Psychological* unfinished business is, of course, always going to be a work in progress. Although temperamentally inclined to be upbeat, I still have to consciously stop myself from keeping digging problems up like a dog with a bone, chewing over what ifs – or worst still, allowing myself to be swayed by well-intentioned leads promising cure ... but for earlier stage or entirely different kinds of cancer!

It is of course just as important to acknowledge what I cannot currently do: I dare not *visualise* the specifics of my dying. In the last 3 weeks, whilst my pain meds have been adjusted I have experienced levels and varieties of pain that defy description. It interrupts thought processes as effectively as throwing a switch and, despite a vast repertoire of pain management techniques, leaves me craving the oblivion of sleep – only to encounter dreams that are filled with sinister foreboding. Yes, *Dignitas* may be an option (note to self – renew passport!) but my vital force is still strong so I sense that what I still have is time.

My conclusion? That it is imperative at this point to "get out of the way!" To explore what my Higher Self is trying to teach me by playing creatively with energies that connect me with the big picture.

*   *   *   *

A course in miracles

From the outset, these musings have been geared to exploring the premise that spiritual experiences are potentially as commonplace as physical, mental and emotional ones, but that we simply don't have the language to convey what is essentially intangible.

If this is the case, as the Dr Patrick MacManaway quotation in the foreword highlights, and we can give ourselves permission to see ourselves as ... *not so much human beings who may choose to walk a spiritual path, but rather spiritual beings who have chosen to walk a human path*, then we will have the confidence to challenge the stranglehold of the "*if you can't touch it, it doesn't exist*" school of thought.

Without owning this aspect of ourselves however we will be condemned to a half-life, unable to achieve our full potential and chasing mirages that appear to promise success but fail to deliver the joy, let alone sense of satisfaction, that is our birth right. This acts as my reminder to centre down to that point of absolute stillness beyond words, where in the comfort to be found in silence I can tap into some other realm entirely and access a more mystical creativity that prompts me simply to "let go and trust".

> *Quakers do have something very special to offer the dying and bereaved, namely that we are at home in silence. Not only are we thoroughly used to it and unembarrassed by it, but we know something about sharing it, encountering others in its depths and, above all, letting ourselves be used by it*
> (Quaker Faith & Practice #17.06)

For me it means resisting the temptation to fill the space with platitudes or becoming distracted by attempts to fix and, rather than any of the myriad forms of "doing", simply "being" – waiting in a state of trust for promptings that come from wisdom beyond our own. I've discovered first-hand what William Penn, an early Quaker who founded Pennsylvania, recorded in 1699:

True silence ... is to the spirit what sleep is to the body, nourishment and refreshment

> (Quaker Faith & Practice # 2.13)

More recently a British Quaker has furnished us with a definition of this "true silence", namely:

> *... not just of sitting still, not just of not speaking, but of a wide awake, fully aware non-thinking. It is in this condition, found and held for a brief instant only, that I have experienced the existence of something other than 'myself'. The thinking me has vanished, and with it vanishes the sense of separation, of unique identity. One is not left naked and defenceless, as one is, for example, by the operations of the mind in self-analysis. One becomes instead aware, one is conscious of being a participant in the whole of existence, not limited to the body or the moment ... It is in this condition that one understands the nature of the divine power, its essential identity with love, in the widest sense of that much misused word*   Geoffrey Hubbard 1974
>
> (Quaker Faith & Practice #26.12)

What's my "story"?

Reviewing the above makes me realise that my goal now needs to be to identify not only the "stuff" that has genuine meaning for me but the beliefs and values that motivate me. Only by explicitly taking stock of my perceptions in this way can I make the conscious shifts in perspective that will put me in a better position to refine my exit strategy by challenging the dross underpinning the belief systems that society imposes on us.

Far from being a luxury I need to examine the minutiae of what, until now, I have simply bought into, in order to convey alternatives that others can also recognise as being credible and valid. If I achieve nothing else in my time remaining, I realise that it is this that will furnish this stage of my life with real purpose – and, what would have once been way off my comfort zone is now an imperative!

By far the strangest outcomes from all of this is the emerging realisation that how I die MAY have the potential to be life-changing for those remaining. I'm experiencing an increasingly desperate need to challenge the stranglehold that science and consumerism have exerted in recent decades, in defining worldly success from a purely financial perspective - and then dictating agendas accordingly. This blinds us to the natural cycles that are demonstrated so emphatically in the UK by the evolving seasons.

"A time to reap and sow, a time to fish or to mend our nets".

How could a death possibly mean "The End" when each year we see bulbs emerging from the frozen earth and seeds germinating where weeks earlier the ground had lain fallow?

My greatest wish would therefore bizarrely no longer be for a pain-free death, though I'm obviously not ruling it out! Just as childbirth is an agony of mess, I'm beginning to suspect that the same occurs in reverse as all the bodily systems shut down. An equal priority would to die in a way that is life affirming, in as much as it demonstrates to those who witness and support me, that it is our spirituality that underpins and drives our physical, mental and emotional selves.

Central to this is the *Vision* that I carry regarding my death, which unlike my dying, is vividly clear to me. Some years ago I was woken in the early hours by the sight of atoms of sunlight dancing so vibrantly across water that the fluidity of their motion produced faint notes of music. This light show probably only lasted for a few seconds, but the accompanying sense of joy and liberation remains. It was so different from a "normal" dream state that I knew immediately that not only had a terminally ill friend died earlier that night and was bidding me farewell, but also that she was en-route to an "afterlife". Less of a "dust to dust, ashes to ashes", as reunion at a quantum physics type level to the star dust of our ancestry and the eternal inter-connectedness of all beings.

Several similar such experiences form the root of my absolute conviction about the existence and continuance of "soul" after the physical body has been shed. These were reinforced when I attended workshops run by Elizabeth Kubler-Ross (one of the pioneers of the hospice movement) and felt the "rightness" of her analogy that we move from this life to the next as inevitably as a caterpillar transforms into a butterfly. Sadness is for those remaining, not for those "graduating".

Since I lack any formal Christian education, concepts such as there being a heaven and hell are a complete anathema. Nor can I buy into the various metaphors of God as a book keeper auditing our sins, critical parent always raising the bar or even grandfatherly figure complete with flowing beard. Instead, what makes sense to me is that life, at least here on Earth, is comprised of an ever-shifting flow of Yin-Yang type energies – so that light and dark are neutral terms conveying simply a never-ending rebalancing whereby harmony can be disrupted or restored.

Put simply, my own faith is an eclectic mix that enables me to find a means of expressing;

- my gut knowledge that I have already experienced many lifetimes

- that we incarnate by choice into forms that allow us to learn lessons relevant to our soul's development and that, in order to do this

- we draw to ourselves situations that we can however choose to either pursue or avoid.

The perspective achieved by facing our shadow side

In general I love the Jungian concept of archetypes, because I find it illuminating to explore how themes from myths and fairy tales resonate with issues we contend with in our own lives and particularly, how our "shadow" self can be our best teacher if we are prepared to befriend rather than repress or deny its messages.

The problem with "real" life however is the number of contradictions. I never realised before encountering the rawness of this situation that I can actually hold two opposing positions simultaneously – and not be on the verge of a breakdown! I can genuinely be grateful beyond measure for each of the acts of love that friends and family spontaneously show me AND incandescent with white hot rage at the careless lack of thought betrayed by an innocent gesture.

So paradoxically, one of the biggest lessons I'm learning is the power of being authentic rather than hiding behind "I'm fine". Just as it was crucial to resist the invitation by patients who assumed I had all the answers to Life because, as a Homeopath, I could hand out advice sheets; I now know better than to pretend that it's possible or even healthy to imagine that I can be upbeat at all times about all aspects of my condition.

In fact I feel a huge sense of responsibility to counter impressions that I'm somehow so highly evolved that I'm immune to all the angst. It feels like another TA "game" with all sorts of hidden agendas, one of the most destructive being the guilt generated by imagining that there is a hierarchy to woe, where death trumps anything else, so friends become too embarrassed to share their own challenges.

My rejoinder is *"it's got to stay a 2 way street!"*. But equally, what follows gives a necessary voice to my "shadow" side, because *Discomfort* appears in a variety of guises:

When I'm not at my best ...

- The exhausting level of organisation required by the something as banal as settling onto my recliner which, in order to anticipate every foreseeable need, is actually closer to the challenge of planning for a major campaign: glasses (for reading and TV!); drink (and straw); protective gear for spills; pens and paper; the phone not tantalisingly just out of reach. Then waiting, whilst the waves of pain abate, so I can breathe again - only to discover that the dog or I then immediately need a "comfort break".

- The dislike of my mean spiritedness when required to be grateful for the very real acts of generosity and goodwill – when my inner critic is shouting "return my calls promptly", "arrive when you say you will", or "apologise when you've clearly forgotten". Certainly "don't arrive unannounced and interrupt the sleep that compensates for my early morning waking, catch me without the psychological protection of "a bit of lippy" or mortified by a room fusty with wet dog – or worse!

- I can't help resenting the implication that since I don't have the same calls on my time, I should appreciate you fitting me into your busy schedule. My own resources are significantly depleted which makes the pressures I face in trying to optimise them different, not less important. I know you don't mind catching me still in my night wear at lunch-time – but I want to maintain a semblance of normality for as long as possible, so it matters to me.

- *"if in doubt, leave me to get on with it myself"* – or better still *"just leave me alone!"* You have no idea what it is like living my life in the equivalent of a fish bowl, constantly on view. So yes, I am aware that it is me who is hyper-alert to being judged when I register your shock at my loss of mobility, changes in appearance and increased dependence. I can only apologise for the Catch 22 that sets your genuine desire to be of assistance against the outcome of rubbing salt into my wounds.

- Biting my tongue because we all do things differently, but really, do you have to choose the option guaranteed to create more work for us all, or make a mountain out of a mole hill ... every time?

- Hating how I look and feel because constant tiredness is causing me to age a decade for every month that passes. This isn't my body anymore, just a series of mechanisms whose actions are becoming increasingly unpredictable

- The fact that there are no answers and after all this time I'm still being caught on the back foot trying to manage basics because the f-ing goal posts have moved yet again!

- Self-pity: what is the point of reading the travel section of the papers now I can no longer leave the house? Or how am I supposed to censor the constant grimness of the news headlines that give undue weight to tales of inhumanity?

Unlike TS Eliot's Prufrock, I find myself *measuring out my life* not *in coffee spoons,* but in the time spent waiting to be ejected from my recliner's gravity field or for people to return with … whatever, having taken a detour involving a delay of a few minutes or an eternity, depending on perspective. Just as *never-to-be-sent letters* help clear the dross, so "a good moan" like this leaves me able at least to smile wryly at myself for getting so wound up.

Having always dreamed in glorious technicolour productions, I also possess an additional route for accessing the gifts from my subconscious. When I recall for instance, my dream of coming home to find my (empty!) willow coffin propped up in plain view on the end of our drive, I realise that I am working out how to "tell" and invite my community to take part in the process, whilst I'm still around to contribute and benefit from the exchanges. Since we play all the parts in the dream, I am simultaneously the tiny, bespectacled boy scout kitted out for his first camp, swaying under the weight of his rucksack yet reaching out for his enormous wheeled suitcase also packed to bursting; and the bemused adult encouraging him to re-think by tenderly reassuring him with "*I promise you won't be needing all that*".

The messages, though assuming different guises are always the same: we have such a tendency to over-complicate new undertakings – and yet, as the following shows, we only have to pay attention to receive constant reminders from the universe that we already have what little we truly need.

Spirit given gifts

When we took the momentous decision to decline surgery I realised that if the definition of happiness is to act in ways that provide us with genuine purpose and meaning, the main goal on my *Bucket List* would simply be to stay ahead of the weeds in the organic veg patch - with the bonus of swapping any surplus goodies for drinks at our local! Achievable irrespective of how much time I had remaining. Not a priority for most people, but 100% consistent with my Quaker values that see us taking responsibility as stewards of Nature's bounty

> We do not own the world, and its riches are not ours to dispose of at will. Show a loving consideration for all creatures, and seek to maintain the beauty and variety of the world. Work to ensure that our increasing power over nature is used responsibly, with reverence for life. Rejoice in the splendour of god's continuing creation.
>
> (Advices & Queries #41)

And, in keeping with how "way opens" when we're in the flow, suddenly I found that having sown a friend's spare seeds from the Heritage Seed Library (varieties close to extinction) and achieved a previously unheard of level of germination, I was in the position to pass on this embarrassment of riches to raise funds for our local Quaker meeting. The simplest of acts, triggered by the initial generosity of the donated seeds, spreading like ripples in a pond, to raise awareness of heavy duty issues yet giving all involved a disproportionate amount of pleasure.

Confirmation for me that the universe does not require us to make dramatic gestures but rather, by being true to our innate gifts we will "be the change" that brings out our own best self and prompts those around us to step up too.

From the reaction of neighbours who see me heaving bags of compost around the garden however, I now realise that our understanding of what it means to be dying is extremely limited: either a last convulsive gasp or a more romanticised, languorous decline holding court from a day bed. Certainly not "all systems go!"

Ironically it has also been immensely healing to hear the more profane responses to our news: *"what a shit hand to be dealt"* ... *"why is it always the f-ing nice ones?"* (the latter flattering though sadly not as accurate as I might like to think!) It captures and validates our own rawness, "names" the discomfort – and as previously illustrated, automatically unblocks the stagnation.

I know from conversations with friends that there are some who are actively envious of my "get out of gaol free" card. Not only those whose quality of life is significantly restricted by chronic pain, a degenerative illness or recurrent and profound mental health problems. But also those who have struggled in abusive relationships, with financial uncertainty, an abiding sense of loneliness or pure despair at the wilful destructiveness committed in their names. For them the gains outweigh the losses; whereas for the vast majority of our friends with children, no time would be anything other than a wrench.

For me now, irrespective of the physical discomfort, the sense of being in control of my own destiny means that I wake each morning in my own bed, looking out on a garden containing an abundant fruit and veg harvest. I am constantly reminded that we each have our place: from the dunnocks and other ground feeders that are taking advantage of the seeds spilled from the dispensers hanging from arches swathed in French beans; to the wild baby rabbit sharing our golden courgettes.

Riches beyond measure with a trellis of yellow and red tomatoes waiting to be baked with our basil, garlic and jalapeno peppers, for winter casseroles; fresh-picked knobbly pink fir apple potatoes dressed simply in butter and a screw of black pepper; crispy cucumbers hanging from a wigwam of our hazel stakes; troughs of assorted lettuce, herbs, carrots and beetroot. Along with an abundance of self-seeded edible and medicinal flowers where pollinators thrive, we enjoy Eden.

It is even easy to track how paradoxically everything is working out better than we might hope, with chance to:

- tie up business affairs

- spend time with family and friends to rebuild bridges and ensure that nothing important is left unsaid
- for self-compassion despite knowledge of careless omissions or deliberate hurts
- for taking stock and realising that the only things remaining on the "bucket list" are achievable in any time remaining
- for giving thanks for being kept safe whilst experiencing the many wondrous elements of a full and (largely) satisfying life

It is actually a no-brainer to count my blessings. Yet people have the strangest response to my situation: *"you're so brave"* or *"I hope I'll be as courageous as you when my time comes"*. There is no recognition that being on the outside looking in literally produces an entirely different perspective where notably, apparent losses become gifts.

It was neither "brave" nor "courageous" to forego surgery plus chemo/ radiotherapy, when a decade of working with patients who had chosen the orthodox route had shown me first-hand what even the surgeons themselves probably are unaware of, because by then they have moved on. Even taking into account that I am obviously not seeing a representative sample, my observation is that in this version "Life" can become a treadmill: of referrals to an ever-widening range of hospital departments; to a revolving carousel of consultants unfamiliar with the case notes and between times a regime of repeat prescriptions, each trying to counter the unwanted effects of the others.

There are of course significant downsides involved in my own choices, but overall it's easy to track how paradoxically everything is working out better than we could have hoped. How can I be bored at not being able to leave the house, when instead all my friends visit me here? ... When each season displays its riches: just as with the coming of Spring, we had the privilege of watching 18 different types of birds building themselves up with the seeds and fat balls we had positioned around the garden in readiness for nesting?

I could mourn the loss of the drive that saw me up, washed and dressed and off to work in 20minutes; but why would I when instead I can savour a leisurely coffee whilst checking emails and review the day's plans with R in the light of the weather, our energy levels and general disposition? Pure luxury! Of course it's also not the retirement we envisaged, so the poignancy is not lost on us. But as meditation teaches, it is less distressing if we observe and then give genuine thanks for what we do have!

*   *   *   *

Which brings us full-circle once more to my initial premise that despite "dark nights of the soul", we are kept safe by our spiritual inter-connectedness by the universal energies that bathe and revitalise us.

Dream sequence 3

I am bored and restless – with no role or understanding of the purpose of our journey. Still subdued by the distress of the previous day I have lost the physical vibrancy I enjoyed when we went ashore; yet restricted by the enveloping darkness from picking out any discernible features as we travel, I am unable to settle within the confines of the boat. I envy the shaman as he stands adjusting the tiller, impervious to my presence as he responds intuitively to the tides and wind, despite the deck shifting alarmingly beneath his feet. Strength and composure emanate from him, which only serve to highlight my own frustration at what I cannot hide is the grossly unappealing inclination to pout like a spoiled child. The

eagle is virtually indistinguishable from the prow, engulfed in mist and spray – again seemingly self-contained, in contrast to my own screaming loneliness. My other self remains wrapped safely in the depths of the boat, apparently oblivious to everything.

Provided with this enforced period for reflection I recognise that I could have done things differently and arrived at in a parallel universe where I'd made all the "right" choices: cared less about the opinion of others; lived adventurously rather than focussing on promotions and mortgage; paid more attention to what makes my soul sing rather than getting lost in "great busyness". I know only too well that despite being filled with the best intentions to invest in state of the art equipment, no amount of gear makes up for the discipline of simply putting in the time and effort each day to practice. The shaman is living proof of this road less travelled – just as the faded-silver tracks of scars demonstrate, his physical strength has been honed in many such storms; whilst the way he moves harmoniously with, rather than against the boat, shows how the years have taught him how to merge seamlessly with the energy of the river's current.

As my resentment grows, so the conditions around us deteriorate and it is almost a relief to feel the drama of the rain lashing against my face and the thrill of having to secure myself with ropes as a precaution against being buffeted as the boat crests ever higher waves. Then, without warning, the adventure takes a sinister turn as I am slammed into the side of the boat and, before I can regain my breath, am hurled into the waves where I proceed to be dragged along in its wake.

Alternatively suffocating, then thrust momentarily to the surface, I am paralysed with fear. The enormity of my situation hits me as physically as the rocks that batter and bruise me as I collide with them, or my shoulder screaming from the force of being wrenched as the ropes force me to keep pace with the boat. And then ... nothing ...

the earth shatteringly simple realisation that I am free to let go and, in doing so, bring an end to it all. The promise of peace is so utterly beguiling I dismiss the guilt of abandoning the others. I can even half convince myself that events are beyond my control as the constant pressure on the ropes causes them to loosen. It is as if the violence is happening to someone else and I am simply a bystander for whom finally, the much longed-for end is in sight.

And equally without warning, at the precise moment that the ropes slip free, my wrists are caught in the implacable grip of the eagle's talons. The shift is so sudden it doesn't even occur to me to struggle as I am deposited effortlessly back on board, before it resumes its position. Shaking with shock I struggle to the prow and rather than resisting me when I lie against its back, I am reassured to feel the eagle adjust its wings to cocoon me. Nestled in the warmth of its downy feathers the river water evaporates from my clothes and my heart beat steadies to match the drum-like vibrations that throb through its frame.

As suddenly as the storm arose, so it abated. We are engulfed in calm. Even better I find myself immensely comforted by the realisation that I have survived some trial – or rather, by the recognition that when my own resources have been utterly drained, that there is a benevolent spirit that safely enfolds me and keeps me on course. The words of the Zen master, Joko, ring out clearly in my mind:

'Life takes place second by second.

Just this.

Just this.

Just this.

We never fully succeed, we just keep trying'

I am struck by the realisation that there is no "right" way I "should" be – I can no more expect to sprout feathers and turn into the eagle than I could follow the life path chosen by the shaman. I wear the scars from my hurts differently: a lifetime's tears transformed into jewels by his mysterious craftsmanship. It is as if only when stripped of everything material that I have gone to such pains to accumulate and staring into apparent annihilation, that I know what it truly means to feel that I have nothing to lose – because there is nothing that I need beyond this. Where only bleak despair had permeated every cell of my being, now I feel light enough to dance across the water, alive with nothing short of pure mischief as I kick up a luminous trail of phosphorous!

Perhaps I am dreaming, because our surroundings seem strangely insubstantial. Is it the sparkle of quartz reflecting and *reflected in the water or have the walls of the cavern given way to reveal the trillion stars of the night sky? Is it the sighing of a barely discernible breeze or can I make out hints of cascading notes of music barely within my range of hearing? Is it wishful thinking that we seem to be engulfed by ever-shifting clouds of entities celebrating my safe keeping and beyond them a light show on a scale with the aura borealis? What is for sure is that my soul now sings and any prior angst dissipates, so even the lingering sense of embarrassment at having been so close to giving up everything without greater persistence, is nothing more than a tender reminder that there is a cost to all of this and I need to be tender with myself.*

Chapter 4:   Pre-flight checks

Part I   *Holistic Health and well-being*

Context

If we wait until we are faced with a crisis before we join the dots in terms of taking responsibility for our own health, then we will be at a major disadvantage when confronting the enormity of designing our personalised version of "a good death".

From hazy memories of flying lessons taken before realising that I lacked the basic maths essential for safely navigating between two compass points, I recall going through a set formula of mechanical checks to ensure the plane would stay together in mid-air. What follows therefore is an equivalent manual for a model of holistic health that will help me assess and ideally improve on my well-being, at the very time I will be at my most vulnerable.

In some ways it has been a relief to note that in the decade since I qualified as a homeopath there has been a distinct shift in consciousness in terms of a growing openness to influences from cultures outside of the western world. There is more familiarity with traditions for instance that make use of the concept of energy centres (chakras) and track energy flow by means of meridians; though it is less widely known that these correspond to what we know in western medicine as the endocrine system. Shown to be scientifically valid, the use of disciplines such as acupuncture for pain relief, are now therefore more readily accepted.

What worries me however is that we're not dealing with a level playing field but rather, that as a result of the impact of media bombardment that requires us to be responsible (AKA "age-defying") patients, we are just as likely to switch off our critical faculties entirely! This is such a well-recognised phenomenon where we abdicate personal responsibility in favour of following "expert" advice; although we know it to be flawed, biased or otherwise unreliable. Hence I found myself despairing equally of the patients who religiously read the information sheet provided with their medication, but then totally discount the risks highlighted on the "it won't happen to me" principle"; and of those who binned it without reading, on the basis that "doctor knows best"!

In terms of conventional health choices, it translates into otherwise rational people risking such things as the unwanted effects of the flu vaccination – even though the vaccine is designed so early in the year that as we found in 2015 there is no guarantee it will be effective against the virus that actually evolves! Or, in the same vein, taking medication on the basis that it "lowers the risk of" .... cardio-vascular disease, late onset diabetes, osteoporosis, the list gets ever-longer; whereas the statins for instance that are prescribed to reduce high cholesterol, involve 6 monthly checks to test for the liver damage they can actually cause!!

Ironically we are now increasingly likely to also eat foods which, like spreadable butters have been modified ostensibly to improve health by reducing the levels of saturated fat, but include hydrogenated fats that are associated with more insidious health risks. Without lavish advertising campaigns, would it even occur to us to use personal hygiene and cosmetic products where the list of ingredients in skin care ranges (for example petrol based derivatives, parabens and sodium lauryl sulphide) include the very irritants that compound the symptoms that they were ostensibly designed to relieve?

The cynical part of me sometimes thinks that this information overload is deliberately orchestrated, so that even if we don't require prescribed meds, as consumers we bounce between manufactured health scares and so called miracle foods. The end product may be good for the economy but simply fills our cupboards with over the counter supplements and cleverly marketed cosmetic products that we stop using once the initial enthusiasm has abated and/ or we have been distracted by the next dramatic revelation. After all, how much mouth wash ("gum disease"), essential minerals ("age-defying–libido-increasing"), digestive enzymes (to regulate the imbalance caused in the gastro-intestinal tract by anti-biotics) and "stress busting" anti-oxidants can one person really need - let alone use? Or, as is notoriously true of inadequately designed vitamin supplements, are we aware that even if we do remember to take them we're more likely to be producing extremely expensive urine than achieving any significant health benefit?

As the following diagram illustrates, the orthodox medical model that defines "health" as simply the absence of disease, falls far short. The various themes attributed to each of the categories have been drawn from a range of "light" to more formal academic sources and/or spiritual writings. So whilst far from comprehensive, they at least provide a starting point: which is, that from an holistic perspective, to be "healthy" means that our mental, emotional, spiritual and physical energies are balanced.

Mental health for
effective decision making
- enhanced creativity
- ability to maintain a sense of perspective
- appropriate levels of stimulation

Physical health
to provide energy for actions

- motivation to exercise
- opportunities for rest + relaxation
- balanced energy levels

A Life Well Lived:

trusting our inner wisdom

- managing change fearlessly to transform ourselves into better, happier people
- celebrating differences + unity
- building resilience + flexibility
- practicing discernment + compassion towards self + others
- inspiration + motivation to achieve our full potential for our own and the greater good

Spiritual well-being
to develop / maintain core values + personal integrity

sense of underlying "meaning" / purpose

"congruence" between behaviour + values

Emotional well-being
to feel secure and valued

- supportive relationships
- emotional "intelligence"
- resilient / optimistic

On a day-to day basis it therefore means what and how we eat for instance will impact on our emotional state, which has a knock on effect on our mental functioning. The grabbed coffee and pastry for breakfast provides the desired sugar and caffeine buzz to kick- start our day, but in keeping with the diagram outlining the *physiological effects of stress* in chapter 3, invariably produces the 11am crash that requires more of the same if we are to keep going. The result? That nutritionally we are running on empty, calling instead on adrenalin to supply our "get up and go".

Then, feeling both physiologically and psychologically driven to continue in this manner, it becomes virtually impossible to regain the perspective required to break the ever-decaying cycle. The premise being that this ultimately impairs our ability to hear the voice of our inner wisdom and so inevitably undermines our ability to behave in an authentic manner in keeping with our core values. The reverse is equally true: living out of step with these core values and beliefs will make it difficult to make healthy choices, which will escalate into feeling ever more emotionally drained, unmotivated and physically under par.

The result is the tragedy of what Socrates described as "the unreflected life", potentially manifesting in physical and emotional insecurity, along with the loss of a coherent sense of meaning and purpose in our lives. In turn, this can only serve to undermine our integrity as we cast around for guidance on how we should live from social conditioning and the market place, rather than honouring the innate knowledge that comes from being grounded by our spiritual roots and having the drive, knowledge and vision to embrace change.

The problem as I see it however is that it is not until crises hit, that we have the motivation to test for instance the effectiveness of our communication skills, to assess the outcomes of our time management strategies or to develop our emotional literacy. Certainly one thing is guaranteed – there has been nothing like the realisation that time is limited, to help me focus on making the most of each remaining day, rather than continuing to pay scant regard to all the lifestyle choices that will keep me in peak condition for as long as possible.

So it is immensely reassuring to read in the standard medical text book that summarises the nature and usage of all the available prescribed medications, that orthodox approaches share these same aspirations:

Palliative care is the active total care of patients whose disease is not responsive to curative treatment. Control of pain, of other symptoms, and of psychological, social and spiritual problems, is paramount to provide the best quality of life for patients and their families. Careful assessment of the symptoms and needs of the patient should be undertaken by a multidisciplinary team

British National Formulary – BNF 60 (bnf.org)

However, because I am hyper-sensitive to the dynamics at work in the patient-practitioner relationship, I smile wryly at the wording of the above which is still based on the assumption that medical expertise is "done unto" the patient.

Thankfully the members of the local palliative care team work from the new health paradigm, that encourages me to play a proactive part in the making of informed decisions consistent with the overall goals of my care plan. Our shared aim is that I remain lucid and independent for as long as possible though; the sad inevitability is that because the range of interventions is so restricted, I am more likely to hear "yes, you are doing everything possible", when what I really want is some magic bullet acquired from their long years working in end of life care. Taking it one step further, my soul's wish would be for them to ask about my well-being, to acknowledge the "big picture"; but simply the hours spent waiting by the phone for them to call back and then the days that pass before they are available to visit, makes it clear that this service is also under-resourced and they simply cannot afford to open that can of worms!

So although back in the "real"(?) world it is undoubtedly the emotional roller coaster triggered by the cancer diagnosis that has been the greatest   challenge; by considering each element in turn but taking physical health care as a starting point here, I can demonstrate how fine tuning these basics makes it possible to produce exponential improvement that benefit us at every level of our being. In doing so it will also make the link between mind and body crystal clear; because after all, if we are experiencing physical pain, we could justifiably be feeling emotionally battered, mentally under-siege and spiritually dislocated.

As I illustrated at the beginning of this chapter however, due to a combination of information overload and active misrepresentation about basic health data, my fear is that we no longer share a common understanding of the benchmarks that enable us to make healthy lifestyle choices. I have therefore included a range of up-dated "Top Tips" advice sheets initially compiled for my homeopathy practise in the Appendix, to provide a base line against which the examples in this chapter illustrate how our every-day needs can morph into something quite different at the stage of palliative care.

This is for two equally important reasons: the first being to provide over-stretched carers with an easily accessed point of reference to simplify the seemingly overwhelming range of choices they face. The aim is to encourage them to prioritise their own needs for adequate nutrition, sleep and emotional nurturing (the oxygen mask analogy); because although only a click away, trawling the web for the same information is simply one step too far.

The second is in keeping with the maxim that *'rules are made for the guidance of wise men and the obedience of fools'.* In this context it is to help readers pick and mix what is relevant to their circumstances, rather than re-inventing the wheel or inadvertently employing strategies that are counter-productive. In my case this applies to the judicious use of alcohol, despite all the official warnings! Without doubt it reduces the amount of pain meds (and therefore additional meds for their side effects) I need to take. It also dramatically improves my joie de vivre, which clearly makes R's life much simpler.

If it then helps avoid investing in expensive products that make false claims, then so much the better.

In all cases however common sense measures should be taken when considering applying them and options discussed with the appropriate healthcare practitioner.

Part II: *Physical health needs*

So for me, going back to basics means safeguarding the three main factors that contribute to my physical well-being, which can be measured by having the energy to undertake activities that make my soul sing. These are: refreshing sleep, that enables cellular repair to take place; a healthy digestive tract, that enables me to best assimilate the nutrients from the food I am eating and effective pain management so that my resources are not depleted by the effort involved in withstanding the very real sense of being battered. Since the latter has a direct knock on effect to the others, this is the first to be considered.

Pain management

Just as Jane Austen observed so astutely in her opening to *Pride and Prejudice It is a truth universally acknowledged, that a single man in possession of a good fortune, must be in want of a wife...*, in the same way, my experience is that it seems to be a given that patients struggling to make sense of contradictory guidance about their use of pain meds, will be in receipt of much unsolicited, well-intentioned but ultimately frustrating advice from all and sundry! It reminds me of a similar complaint made by first time parents desperate to do the right thing by their baby but overwhelmed by the sheer weight of literature on the subject, everyone they meet weighing in with their opinion and befuddled by sleep deprivation. In fact I am more likely to be reduced to tears by the resulting Catch 22, as by the pain itself – it sometimes feels as if people think I am wilfully causing my own suffering rather than faced with major "No-Wins".

A case in point:
Analgesics are more effective in preventing pain than in the relief of established pain; it is important that they are given regularly (BNF)

Which I take to mean advises that they should be repeated at specific intervals pre-agreed with my GP. But, this implies that I could well be taking meds even though I am not experiencing any discomfort – on a "just in case" basis.

Then set this against:
- the commonly experienced side effects from even mild analgesics, that can make the trade-off afforded by the pain relief a high price to pay

- the recognition that their effectiveness reduces with use, so as with any drugs more frequent repetition and ultimately higher potencies will be required to maintain the same effect - associated with an equivalent increase in even more debilitating symptoms

- the fact that there are a variety of self-help strategies including low impact exercise, relaxation exercises and massage with essential oils that in some cases can be equally if not more effective, with no adverse trade-offs; or at the very least reduce the range and amount of drugs required

An exercise that IS safe to try at home:

Step 1: sit quietly with an ice cube in your hand until it melts
Step 2: take another ice cube but occupy yourself with conversation, activity etc until it has melted

Spoiler alert! The first quickly becomes excruciating, the second is infinitely easier to tolerate. Consistent with this and in a massive understatement, my student physiology text book notes: *The sense of pain is complex because it involves not only sensation but feelings and emotions as well* (Kapit, Macey + Meisami). Hence the only too familiar experience of toothache disappearing in the dentist's chair, but returning at night when our brain blows it out of all proportion. They then go on to highlight the inconvenient truth that (despite the implicit message promoted by the manufacturers of pain meds) we still have no finite model for understanding pain reception and, more importantly, struggle to comprehend the mechanisms by which the transmission of pain signals are suppressed.

The latest thinking is that there are 2 pain systems: (Ascending Pain Pathways https://thebrain.mcgill.ca/index.php).

A-delta: accounts for the initial localised short lasting, sharp sensation (caused for instance by stubbing a toe); *Type* C: follow with a dull, aching more diffuse pain. Interestingly, this may explain why the offer to "rub it better" (*afferent pain inhibition*) provides more than psychological comfort, because the action overloads the brain with tactile stimulation that is thought to exclude the weaker type of pain signals. More relevant to my situation is the process by which the brain releases neurotransmitters in the form of endorphins (specifically *enkephalin*) to suppress the transmission of pain signals by binding with opiate receptors found within the brain synapses.

Although the precise mechanism is unclear (decreasing the amount of substances released by *type C pain* or inducing *postsynaptic inhibition of the relay cells*?); the key is that morphine and other opiate analgesics act in the same way to cancel out the pain experience. Though highly addictive, this is largely irrelevant when it comes to their use in palliative care!

In my case I experience 4 different sources of pain which vary in terms of frequency, intensity and duration of episodes:

- stabbing, bursting sensations caused by the location of the tumour which obstructs lymph drainage in an area rich with nerve endings. It reduces mobility, prevents me from sitting and occasionally causes me to unexpectedly yelp with shock even when stationary

- inflammation in the surrounding area due to the swelling created by fluid retention, that is acutely sensitive to the pressure of clothing and furthermore shifts excruciatingly with any change in position, causing me for instance to wake each time I turn over in bed

- acute burning on urination due to the chafing and rawness in an area typically warm and moist

- the discomfort that comes from the aching neck and shoulder muscles and pelvic misalignment caused by walking and lying awkwardly to accommodate the tumour

The complexity, intensity and yet changeability of these individual symptom pictures is compounded when taken in combination and illustrates why they are so challenging to redress. Although I am assured that it is reasonable to expect that a split daily dose of morphine should enable me to be completely pain free for the majority of time; my experience to date is that this comes at the cost of side effects that create a constant state of dizziness and nausea associated with significant abdominal discomfort due to the total loss of peristalsis (the action that causes food to progress along the digestive tract).

Recognising the importance of the "use it or lose it" principle driven by the surprisingly rapid deterioration in muscle tone amongst those whose day is broken up by ever-increasing bouts of sleep; being well enough to continue to garden has been my saving grace. After a morning spent feeding prunings from our orchard into a wood chipper for instance, I realised that the bending, stretching and carrying involved had given the lymph glands and section of the digestive tract located in my abdomen a thorough work out. Better still, although being entirely pain free had caused me to completely forget to take one course of tablets, I suffered no ill-effects later in the day and achieved truly refreshing sleep without any sinister drug-induced dreams.

Natural pain relief strategies:

- drinking plenty of fluids keeps urine diluted and, assisted by daily, home- made fresh vegetable juices, bowels open without the need to strain

- a cold gel pack can sometimes reduce the heat of the inflammation (but can also make it worse)

- scrupulous personal hygiene – motivated by reading in the BNF that "rescue" doses of fast relief morphine should be taken 30 minutes before changes of dressing, making it too high a price to pay for the promise that they contain odour cancelling antibiotics

- discovering organic creams and emollients that successfully heal rather than simply control areas of raw skin and are the most wonderful products for anything from self-massage to formal reflexology treatments

- lemon myrtle essential oil and soap that leaves a wonderful fragrance after use, providing an out of proportion psychological boost due to the relief of knowing that visitors will detect no "sick room" stuffiness

- investing in a mattress topper that provides a buffer layer of additional support but without the restrictions (and heat!) generated when lying on posture-form mattresses

- sharing the bed with my Lab-Alsation cross: I initially thought she was actively providing some form of telepathic healing but have worked out that it is just as likely that by sleeping in the crook of my knees she prevents my free movement and hence the pain that comes from constantly adjusting position; whilst her snoring is both reassuring and gives me a rhythm to copy that calms by slowing my own breathing rate

Healthy Eating   Appendix *"Healthy eating"* ...

> *the doctor of the future will give no medicine but will interest his patients in the care of the human frame, in diet, and in the cause and prevention of disease*   Thomas A Edison

The food we eat supplies the vitamins and minerals essential for all life's processes (growth, repair and to activate almost all chemical reactions) in a natural and well-balanced form, that cannot be duplicated as effectively by chemical supplementation. In contrast, many commercially available food items contain a cocktail of additives and preservatives geared to improving appearance, disguising poor quality and extending shelf life. Labelling continues to be misleading and guidance regarding food standards inadequate.

This makes it particularly difficult for patients with chronic health care conditions to design a diet that reduces the toxic load on the organs of elimination (especially urinary tract, bladder and kidneys; liver and gastro-intestinal system). Even though I do not have to contend with the nausea and vomiting associated with chemo and radiotherapy, my own challenge is to manage the severe constipation caused by the pain medication; since it causes the peristaltic motion that "keeps everything moving", to stop functioning.

Because I am convinced that in addition to satisfying basic physical needs, the action of eating provides a vast range of social and psychological benefits, I view it as an essential factor in enhancing the quality of palliative care. What follows therefore is a crash course in nutritional science in an attempt to debunk myths and misinformation about healthy eating and enable both carers and patients to optimise their well-being

Rules of thumb:

For good reason, the maxim "everything in moderation" is a valid starting point when it comes to healthy eating in general...

- fibre supplies the "roughage" that controls the transit time of foods through the digestive system, so that nutrients can be absorbed and toxins eliminated promptly
    - of these, beans and pulses are a major and inexpensive source of complex carbohydrates, protein and essential minerals / fatty acids.

- whole grains are also a rich source of vitamins, minerals and plant chemicals (whereas, once processed, carbohydrates such as white flour and rice will lose the majority of their essential minerals eg up to 98% of chromium, 77% of zinc)

- water - approximately 70% of the human body is water. To be at our best adults therefore need to absorb on average 2.5 Litres of fluid per day, which will be recycled and ultimately lost via urine (1.5L); 700ml(breathing); 200ml (sweat); 100ml (faeces)

- the colours in plant foods relate to the different phytochemicals they contain, each of which has particular health benefits. Eaten daily in different combinations, they act as anti-oxidants that will "mop up" free radicals (cancer forming cells)

- eating a diverse diet also reduces over-exposure to common foods that have been linked to adverse health reactions including asthma, eczema, psoriasis and arthritis. The worst offenders are wheat, dairy produce, citrus fruits, corn, yeast

- diets high in red meats create very strong acids that take about 5 days for the body to clear through the kidneys, after neutralising with alkaline minerals such as calcium

- such diets are therefore associated with gout, urinary infections and osteoporosis (because it involves diverting calcium from bone formation)
- increasing % intake of fruit and vegetables therefore not only exceeds the minimum RDA (recommended daily allowance) of 5 portions (of 80g or equivalent to a palm size) a day, but helps the body fluids remain within the optimum pH range (ie slightly alkaline)

- the benefits of eating foods containing Essential Fatty Acids (EFAs also bring about improvement in skin conditions; lowered blood pressure; and increased functioning of the nervous and immune systems.

Beware:
Counting calories as a guide to healthy eating:

- A chocolate bar may well have less calories than an avocado

- fats are responsible for imparting flavour therefore "low fat" foods will be higher in calories due to the extra salt and/or sugar required to make them palatable

- the concept of "empty calories" ie minimal nutritional value but high in calories, is overlooked by advertisers keen to mobilise children's "pester power" for e.g. breakfast cereals - completely at odds with the Government's stated goal in tackling the "epidemic" of childhood obesity.

The over-simplification of "good" versus" "bad" cholesterol.

Diets rich in saturated fats (dairy and meat products) contain high levels of LDL (low density lipoproteins ie "bad cholesterol") that can cause the arteries to clog and increase the risk of heart disease. Unsaturated and polyunsaturated fats (oily fish, nuts, seeds and their oils) contain essential fatty acids and HDL (High Density Lipoproteins ie "good cholesterol") that are essential in the formation and functioning of cellular tissues, brain function and vision.

Methods of food production and preparation

- intensive farming methods aimed to increasing yield involve heavy investment in pesticides and produce crops that have significantly lower amounts of essential minerals hence the importance of sourcing local produce grown ideally to organic standards

- processed foods have had much of the natural fibre removed and will therefore release sugars faster into the blood stream, causing dramatic swings in moods as well as energy levels.

The chart of low glycaemic index foods is an invaluable indicator of those foods providing slow release energy.

The issue of supplementation is generally oversimplified.

Poor quality supplements for instance fail to provide nutrients in forms that can be absorbed by the body, so that, for example, drinks containing probiotics are unlikely to survive transit through stomach acid in order to benefit the digestive tract.

In addition essential minerals (those that the body cannot manufacture) interact as a complex web, where the assimilation of one will enhance or impair the absorption of others. This explains why we are advised to take iron tablets with fruit juice, because vitamin C enhances uptake. Calcium supplements (prescribed to offset the risk of osteoporosis) however will block receptors of its "partner" Phosphorous as well as increase the risk of forming kidney stones

Whereas daily exposure to sunlight (20 minutes) increases the production of retinol and hence Vitamin D which aids the absorption of calcium, which is also available in a wider range of foods other than dairy products

Fluid intake

Although we would die faster from lack of water than from starvation, there are also cases where people suffering for instance with urinary tract symptoms have drunk so much water in an attempt to flush out the infection that they have died. Other issues to be aware of are:

- fizzy drinks may increase the risk of weakened bones - possibly because the body diverts calcium to neutralise the acidity produced by the carbon dioxide "fizz" from its essential role in bone formation or the phosphorous content of the drinks alters the delicate balance of minerals in the body and causes calcium to be broken down. Irrespective of the reason, 1/5th of fizzy drink addicts were found to have suffered fractures before the age of 20

- caffeine (also found in cola and "high energy" drinks, medications e.g. Lemsip) and alcohol, not only deplete the body of essential nutrients but encourage dehydration

- tea drinkers however have stronger bones than non-tea drinkers, which suggests that the fluoride and flavonoids ie plant chemicals contained in tea that act as anti-oxidants, promote bone density (whilst added milk produced even higher bone mineral density, particularly in the hip area!)

Refreshing Sleep

Most people need a minimum of 8 hours sleep per night to provide the opportunity for our physical and mental systems to rest, repair and renew themselves. Recent research has shown that losing a mere 1/2hour each night results in reduced academic performance, increased moodiness and even the likelihood of obesity.

- Avoid caffeine (found not only in coffee, but also cola drinks, chocolate, tea etc) and other stimulants (including alcohol and sugary foods) at least throughout the evening

- Don't eat a heavy meal too close to bedtime because the effort required to digest it will reduce the quality of your sleep But also beware of going to bed hungry – some people find a warm drink e.g. milk particularly soothing

- Make your bedroom a place to sleep – if you study, watch TV or play video games there, take a break before getting ready for bed to allow your brain chance to unwind

- If pain keeps you awake, find natural remedies (e.g. to reduce inflammation) wherever possible to support your body's attempts to heal and make sure your mattress, pillows etc are not making the problems worse

- If you find your brain is buzzing with ideas, make a list of everything and keep a pad and pencil beside the bed in case you wake. This gives your brain permission to switch off rather than worrying about forgetting something

- Make sure your body is warm (bed socks and a hot water bottle may not be exciting but are essential if your feet are like icebergs); but that your room is cool, quiet and as dark as possible (even the light from your alarm clock can trick your body into thinking it is time to wake). For the same reason, if you need to get up in the night for the loo, try to avoid putting the main light on – but don't fall down the stairs!

- Establish a routine at night that encourages you to wind down: e.g. a bath is more relaxing than a shower; read a magazine or listen to soothing music. Go to bed and wake at the same time
- Sleep aids include earplugs, lavender essential oil (a few drops sprinkled on your pillow or nightwear)

- If you find yourself getting agitated because you are unable to sleep, try visualisation and other relaxation exercises counting your breaths and consciously slowing them down (e.g. feet breathing)

- Since emotional upset in particular can result in disturbed / unrefreshing sleep, nightmares etc seek counselling or other help to identify and redress any unresolved issues – R always said we should never go to sleep on an argument! And we never did.

A love letter to myself

My dearest Chris,

This is the place to turn to when you have lost sight of the things that bring you joy and instead, 'compassion fatigue' is making you "sick and tired of feeling so sick and tired"! It's a reminder of what you want to achieve and its place in 'the Big Picture'. So STOP! Make yourself a drink, get comfortable and take time out to read this with the attention it deserves.

Take stock: whatever else has been happening, you only ever get this low when you're over-tired, so what has caused the build up?

Over-riding warning signals? You're prone to getting on the "should, must, ought" hamster wheel, so re-check priorities and cancel anything that doesn't make your soul sing – Or, change your perspective so a "chore" becomes a pleasure or earns you a treat. You love the sight of a line full of washing, the air-dried fragrance of clean laundry and the luxury of slipping between fresh sheets. It just doesn't have to be done to-day!

If it's the anti-climax after having friends to stay, then 'name' the mix of emotions that have been evoked. Chat to an empty chair if there were things left unsaid or unfinished – then swap to 'listen' to what your inner wisdom can reveal that will help reconcile you to what is and isn't realistic in terms of outcomes

It may simply be that thunder storms have caused Bonny to repeatedly wake you, building works have made a siesta impossible or you're going through another phase of early morning waking / unrefreshing sleep because your dreams are so frantic

In any case, bite the bullet and do what it takes to make sure you can sleep the clock around until you've caught up again. Bliss!

Keep track of achievements and the little things that mean a lot. You've noticed that for each accidental hurt received, it has coincided with a gift of such astounding generosity that you've been struck by how many people are walking the extra mile with you. So yes, it's absolutely fine to whinge (or rant), just don't dump on others and most of all 'call time' so that it doesn't leak into the fun stuff.

Consider whether:

 events have conspired to rub salt into the wounds related to loss of independence and vitality

you're not feeling heard

you're physically under-par so finding it hard to concentrate, struggling to recall important details (have I taken the pain meds?)

You may be Taurean and stubborn ++ but you know that you can't force your body to "behave" simply by the force of your will power. You can however target the following areas and achieve exponential results:
Digestion – improved ability to assimilate nutrients and eliminate toxins
Rebalance hormones – particularly adrenal overload
Support immune function + reduce inflammatory responses
Restore refreshing sleep
Adjust lifestyle to reduce stress factors
Improve emotional wellbeing and reduce mood swings

Equally there are specific times / triggers that you can anticipate and develop strategies to deal with to ultimately help you feel more in control eg:

-you're always zonked out after eating because of the energy involved in the digestive processes, so unless you're feeling unduly agitated this is NOT the time to fret about low G-I diets and caffeine intake - you'll benefit from the hour of energy they buy you in order to be on form for visitors or to indulge in a burst of creativity

ensure daily elimination because the morphine makes you particularly susceptible to 'motility issues' and you want at all costs to avoid the mouth fug of toxicity and the sensation that the Alien is about to burst forth

remind R that your appetite is as erratic as during pregnancy so "less is more" to avoid being over-faced and let him know of any cravings so he feels his efforts to locate treats are rewarded

having a wide flavour of fluids available will relieve symptoms of nausea (eg fresh ginger, fennel), lemon water will support the liver's efforts to detox and you find the spic mixes in Ayurvedic teas particularly comforting

stay active – it's more than "use it or lose it", it's about the feel good hormones that get released when you're out in nature, the sense of achievement that gardening produces, just as much as the bending and stretching that gives the digestive system the work-out it needs to keep things moving

You're good at pacing yourself: using the 70-30 rule to replace the equivalent of an emotional / physical "overdraft" , but I appreciate how frustrating it is trying to gauge how to stop when 30% of energy remains, when even lying quietly in a darkened room is a drain. Rather than having to cancel longed-for events, Ration visits and phone calls and supplement with emails that can be edited for several different recipients. You still get the glow of the connection. And with R agreeing to go away for his own respite a few days each month, you have the luxury of re-establishing your own rhythm and making headway with your art projects.

The roller-coaster of highs and lows are inevitable as you deal with the intensity, duration and frequency of symptoms. PLEASE don't add to you load with negative self -talk. Yes, you have been "robbed" and there are no "magic bullets". Life for you and R has changed immeasurably but whatever lies ahead there will be options and solutions (that others can suggest if they're only invited!) Live in the moment and know that you are profoundly loved.

YOU'RE A STAR – shine on!

Part III Resilience: *Emotional literacy*

Emotional well-being to feel secure and valued

- supportive relationships
- emotional "intelligence"
- resilient / optimistic

Without doubt, the most challenging part of dying is managing my own and others' raw emotions. So in terms of compiling this holistic health jig-saw I am undoubtedly blessed that my professional training has provided both the theoretical and experiential framework to explain the bi-polar swings from homicidal rage to abject self-pity that periodically engulf me.

This has and still is, being constantly refined through membership of the Religious Society of Friends (Quakers) with their unshakeable commitment to peace, along with other readings about models of non-violence.

As a result I do my very best not to beat myself up with negative self-talk, as well as to give others the benefit of the doubt by assuming their intentions are genuinely sincere, irrespective of outcome. Though the "snippy" rejoinder of "I'm not pregnant" to friends fussing about whether for instance I should be helping to carry out the garden seating is never far from the tip of my tongue - I can at least soften it with a smile!

Underpinning this balancing act is the commonly held concept that some emotions are positive whilst others are "negative". As a psychologist, Steve Biddulph in *The secret of happy children* however suggests a refreshingly different approach:

> *"In their pure form, emotions are distinctive sets of body sensations, which we experience under specific situations. They range from subtle to very strong in intensity. They are constantly with us – flowing and merging together as we resolve each event in our life and move on. We are always feeling something – emotions are a symptom of being alive!"*

He takes this further, saying that there are only 4 main emotions:

ANGER   FEAR   SADNESS   JOY

Any other emotions are arguably a mixture of these basic feelings, so that Jealousy for instance could be said to be a mix of Anger plus Fear. Rather than a "failing" that culturally we are conditioned to suppress, each is in fact vital for our survival. By using the technique of accurately "naming" the first three it is possible to defuse their negative potential; which leaves us with the Joy that comes from a sense of restored emotional equilibrium. From this perspective it is easier to see the big picture and in turn, we foster the more mystical sensation of being connected with a resource beyond our conscious awareness on which we can draw when our own strengths are depleted.

Although members of religious groups may face an additional challenge due to the admonishment to "turn the other cheek", this overlooks for instance the outrage that fuelled Jesus when he drove the moneylenders out of the temple. There is a time and place for everything as long as we are alert to the danger of damaging others by our lack of awareness about the impact of our thoughts and actions.

Quakers in particular recognise that our testimony to peace creates huge difficulties for us as individuals and as an organisation in dealing with all forms of conflict; so have produced much helpful literature that underpins quite astounding pioneering work in projects from schools to war zones, using non-violence and mediation to achieve reconciliation between opposing factions.

I am therefore extraordinarily grateful to have recently been granted (better late than never!) one of those insights that arrives like a lightning strike of realisation, but on reflection is almost embarrassingly self-evident!

Namely that there is a world of difference between allowing ourselves to fully experience these emotions and thereby recognise their validity – but this does not give us carte blanche to inflict them on those around us who are unwittingly caught up in the fall-out zone. Instead, as we see with survivors of unimaginable tragedy, when they can channel all the distress and losses positively into projects that prevent or support others through similar experiences; it helps them restore meaning and purpose to lives changed irrevocably by forces beyond themselves.

Yet because conditioning runs deep: *"big boys don't cry"* ... *"nice girls don't get angry"*, we all need permission to conclude instead that emotions are simply another form of energy - like electricity, they are invisible but their effects can be clearly be seen and felt! This is why we enjoy being in the company of some people, whilst others "drain us". When emotions become blocked we will also experience physical symptoms of stress, so it's no surprise to find that research has discovered that the reverse holds true and safely discharging this build-up of tension is a crucial step, especially in pain management.

As my experience with the consultant illustrated so very vividly, **ANGER** is a justifiably strong and passionate emotion triggered by a sense of injustice. As a primary response it indicates fierce displeasure. Significantly however it can also be a secondary emotion arising in that instance from my fear and embarrassment; but equally from disappointment, frustration or sorrow. Handled appropriately its purpose is to make us stand up for ourselves, so is vital for self- preservation and freedom. Sadly and despite my best intentions R tends to be on the receiving end of its more familiar cousins, bickering and nagging; behaviours created when the emotional gloop remains undifferentiated and rather than cleanly discharged, leaks like a toxic cloud!

SADNESS is a physiological necessity because the chemical changes that accompany grief literally wash us clean of the distress caused by the loss of someone or something. We therefore do ourselves and others no favours for instance by trying to prescribe the "appropriate" length of time spent grieving; though there are no shortage of people who tell themselves within the

first (and subsequent) year(s) following a bereavement
that "I should be over this by now".

> *People so often talk of someone "getting over a death".*
> *How could you ever fully get over a deep loss? Life has*
> *been changed profoundly and irrevocably. You don't get*
> *over sorrow; you work your way right to the centre of it.*
>
> Diana Lampen 1979 (Quaker Faith & Practice #17.06)

Tragically this insight is pretty useless when R is
consumed throughout his waking hours by the "what ifs"
and "if onlys", that ricochet around his head like wasps in
a jar or that clutch his chest in a vice making the simple
act of breathing a major effort. The biggest surprise is the
full-on impact of "anticipatory grieving", since everything
we do (but with the advent of warm weather particularly
the fun stuff like BBQs) serves to remind him that all this
is time limited and he will be managing alone in a matter
of months. It is like having the bad fairy busting in on
Sleeping Beauty's christening party!

As if this isn't enough, there is simultaneously a type of
"survival guilt" that stems from the difference in our
genetic codes and the expectation that, like his own
parents, he can anticipate a further fifteen to twenty
years of robust good health. But the simple knowledge
that he has a safety net for filtering out "stuff" until he is
in a better position to deal with it, confirms his trust in

the innate wisdom of "*a time for everything and everything in its time*".

Although *Meet me where I am,* illustrates that the losses I am experiencing are probably more apparent to visitors than to me, with "*time to stand and stare*" being as guilty a pleasure as any chocolate goody; dreams may show that I'm not exactly processing the changes as smoothly as this! Lots of frantic train journeys where I've lost the purse containing my ticket; barely getting to safety before an avalanche hits; caught up in traffic jams; rooms with doors made of glass and with locks that don't work ... it doesn't take a genius to recognise the desperate amount of paddling that is going on beneath this swan's unruffled exterior!

In turn we are managing our **FEAR** because "denial" ably assisted with generous quantities of alcohol (well a glass or two of Baileys or white wine) allows us to break down the impenetrable cloud that hangs over us into manageable chunks.

Fear gives us the opportunity to first spot the potential threat – if I am in severe pain what can be done? Analyse potential options – increased medication, hospital care, hospice respite (?) and, by anticipating a range of scenarios, seek the least damaging alternative.

I don't like to think of my death as being the gross and horribly painful process threatened by the consultant; but I'm grateful that this possibility has been flagged up from the outset, rather than finding myself slipping insidiously towards it.

Fear of this has prompted us to plan ahead. So I now grab, with both hands, for instance, the tentative offers made by those with nursing experience to oversee pain meds and, if need be, provide compassionate personal care. Thus, guaranteeing the preservation of my dignity whilst buffering R, as much as possible, from harsh realities.

The resulting peace of mind is crucial, because I also learned from Transactional Analysis that just as there are a series of life stages we all go through as we navigate from dependence to independence towards becoming mature adults (with varying degrees of success!); these then play out in reverse. So that, as we age increasing frailty will, if left to run its course, bring a return of the "mewling babe" dependence depicted in Shakespeare's *Seven ages of man*. This prospect is so appalling to me as a previously robust woman proud of being a feisty free spirit.

But again serendipity has provided me with a useful "dry run" when six years ago it was incredibly hard for me to tolerate the various indignities that breaking my leg and being confined to a wheel chair involved. In fact, because I am currently still mobile, the experience has helped me actually appreciate many of my small yet significant, hard-won everyday achievements like preparing meals and gardening; which were major challenges even when I was promoted to crutches. Until then I hadn't realised how much distance was covered collecting the ingredients and then transferring them between, fridge, sink and oven; nor the contortions involved in accessing shelves and cupboards.

Carers be(a)ware! It is impossible to convey the head space that it takes to anticipate every eventuality so that energy can be used most effectively; motivated by the knowledge that it is still easier than trying to explain what needs doing.

I'm constantly astounded at how an apparently shared language unravels to gobble-d-gook when requests such as *"pass me a dish"* result in the production of bowls, platters – in fact everything but! As I frequently explain to R, it's not that I'm short-tempered, more, that I'm seriously provoked! Not that my way is the only right way, but with the goal of energy conservation each activity needs to be planned and executed efficiently. Fortunately I've mellowed since my plate throwing days – or maybe its enforced pragmatism since such tantrums would be a dreadful waste of my disposable energy reserves...

In conclusion therefore, it occurs to me, in fact, that emotions are like our children – a product of our life choices. We can scrutinise their every move and for sure their behaviour will become more outrageous and disruptive; or we can focus on the positives and thereby elicit more of the same. This isn't the naively dangerous psycho-babble implicit in the mantra *we create our own reality* - which by implication means that I've been guilty of some major negativity in wishing this cancer on myself. Rather that there is some scientifically verifiable force or even a spiritual lore at work whereby *"energy follows attention"*.

JOY: experienced when all the above emotions have been met

Margaret Torrie, the founder of Cruse counselling service for the bereaved, confirmed that there is a predictably consistent series of processes that we follow before life can resume a semblance of normality

> *There are clearly marked signposts which, if followed, lead the way to recovery. First there has to be the wish, however transient, to find the way to better things. It is the beginning of hope, that basic ingredient for all life. From there, confidence and belief develop, and the certainty that despite all evidence to the contrary, good is in us and around us, offering support... Our own willingness to love and give in the world about us is the secret of recovery and the new beginning.* (1970)
>
> Quaker Faith & Practice #22.90

My joy ultimately lies in the fact that I know for me the outcome will be a new beginning. And in trusting that those I leave behind will ultimately experience the joy of our life together and after the sadness and grief, anger and fear has abated know that energy and love never dies.

Part IV: Spirituality and other useful tools

Om Namah Shivaya

I honour the Divinity that resides within me

From an holistic perspective to be "healthy" simply means that the interaction between our mental, emotional, spiritual and physical energies are (largely) in balance. Whether we refer to the resulting state as 'being in the zone' or attribute it 'our higher self', 'inner wisdom', 'universal energy' or 'god'; the outcome is unambiguous, it *will bring us towards ever greater experiences of joy and peace.* Then, if as Dr Patrick MacManaway's quotation suggests, we are indeed *spiritual beings who have chosen to walk a human path,* indicators of 'a life well-lived' are presumably not to be found in outward signs of success but rather the sense of congruence we achieve between our daily activities and the contribution these make to the betterment of our world.

I have had much time to reflect on career paths, opportunities (largely missed) for creative self-expression and given the dire state of the environment, whether I could / should have committed with greater urgency to various forms of social activism. I have concluded however that these questions are as much of a red herring as it would have been to chase financial rewards or other symbols of material success, or devoting myself to pure hedonism. It is not that I believe that our fate is predetermined, but rather that whether we are a rocket scientist or nomad, events will unfold in our lifetime that give us the opportunities to play out different scenarios that allow our unique spiritual journey to continue to unfold.

The familiar symbol depicting Yin and Yang energies, encapsulates the constant state of flux that is entailed as we adapt and respond optimally to the ever-changing environment in which we find ourselves. Whether viewing it as what western scientists term "homeostasis", Traditional Chinese Medicine as the shifting dominant – passive, male-female energies or, as with psychoanalytical models the inter-play of unconscious and conscious psyche; the resulting fluidity enables us to remain "in the flow", whilst withstanding "Life's slings and arrows".

Although there is general agreement that the resulting balance and harmony is transient, only achieved through fleeting glimpses, there are undoubtedly elements that we can set in place that make it more, or less, accessible. My sense is that these are closely allied with what we experience through mysticism: the acknowledgement of an inter-connectedness with a universal force that inspires creativity, is easier to find in Nature than in concrete jungles and achieved more readily through a playful lightness of being rather than a dour intensity of intellect.

This is undoubtedly the state that I aspire to in my quest for "a good death" and paradoxically I currently find myself healthier now, despite the diagnosis of 'a life limiting illness', than I was this time last year when contending with several months of post viral malaise and the disquiet felt in the deepest level of my being that "all was far from well". This is not simply my impression but confirmed by the various complementary therapists who are supporting me. They attribute it to the dramatic reduction in stress levels that comes with being forced by events that cannot be changed, into letting go:

> There isn't some ideal way you are meant to be all day.
> The fact is, you are the way you are.
> Just being aware of how you are,
> without self-judgement, repression or analytical scrutiny,
> in itself changes something.
> Accept your feelings and gradually they work their way out.
> That's all we can do
> Joko Beck Zen master

In these last months I have learned that:

- dying is not simply a matter of marking time waiting for the other shoe to drop, but is instead a genuinely exciting process filled with the prospect of the gifts that each new day brings; in appreciating the paths that continue to open, along with the new skills and learning that these usher in

- no magic bullet exists that will eradicate the amount of pain I am experiencing at any given time, but I can certainly learn to surf through the highs and lows and manage the factors that will alleviate it or make it worse (dehydration, unrefreshing sleep, poor posture, unhealthy diet)

- my attitude undoubtedly affects the degree of ease with which I can navigate through each day, because "energy follows attention". So if I indulge in playing "poor me", for sure I will make life as miserable for myself as those around me. Or, I can pay attention to the sense that every time I get served a lemon (the latest being to receive a 3 page email "dumping" angst! Why!!!), there is an act of breath-taking generosity that brings a glow as if all the non-material spirits in the universe are smiling on me (the very same day's surprise visit from the neighbour's children, dropping in to introduce their new puppy)

As the Joko Beck Zen quotation illustrates however, the 'biggie' has been to lay to rest my own preconceptions with how I should be *without self-judgement, repression or analytical scrutiny.* I had no idea how critical my self-talk tends to be, nor how much my self-worth was (maybe still is) tied up with the embarrassingly superficial preoccupations about my appearance, intellect and vitality. Part of this is definitely associated with what friends have repeatedly pointed out is a misplaced desire to protect them – assuring me that it is for them to find ways to deal with their own reactions to whatever takes place during visits. Confirmed by the realisation that they barely register the adaptations I have needed to make in order to remain independent, because in their words *"it's still the same 'me' that continues to shine through"*.

So now that energy has to be portioned out and priorities set accordingly, it has been such a relief to let go of some of the driving and striving – not compromising but rather distilling down to pure essence. Although it is undoubtedly still a struggle to maintain eye contact with my ageing mirror image, I can bear to ask what there is to not like in what I see. By refusing to chase an arbitrary, culturally imposed ideal of perfection and thereby submitting myself to the implicit process of evaluation and judgement that this entails; I automatically defuse the despair and consequent raft of anxieties that accompany the inevitable sense of having "fallen short" of the ideal. In doing so, this is when I discover the totally unexpected: that this acceptance *in itself changes something* – and for the better.

But this is undoubtedly on a good day...

Dark nights of the Soul

After the euphoria that characterised the first few months following the diagnosis, in this latter stage of my illness and especially when pain management slips, I disappear for 2-3 days into what some term "the dark night of the soul".

Apparently it can be most pronounced amongst those who have a strong religious faith, when they are suddenly and unaccountably robbed of the ability to sustain themselves with the prayerful upholding that has been their trusty safety net through past adversity.

For me it is the time when the battering I am experiencing could so easily be projected onto those around me, even though I am desperate in the face of my own rawness to avoid as far as possible becoming the petulant and manipulative type of patient. It is the time when there is a very real temptation to play the "death card" as a means of carelessly discharging the layers of hurts, wilfully indifferent to the impact of those in the fall-out zone. A sort of V-sign to the world that feeling shitty justifies behaving like it too.

The first encounter with this craving for oblivion coincided with the total exhaustion that overtook me whilst undertaking the gate keeping processes from GP to oncology surgeon and what, with hindsight was the impact of the malevolent force of the latter's threat of "a long and painful death".

It is shocking but relatively commonplace to hear how promptly patients can die after hearing their diagnosis, like both of my parents failing to achieve the months if not years that the medics anticipated. Tragic too to note the number of websites that have sprung up listing the various damaging statements that medics repeatedly make and the effort required by already-debilitated patients to reverse their impact.

Although seemingly far-fetched, in fact, I learned when working within the Afro-Caribbean community in south London that mental health problems there often arose after a person discovered that they had been "cursed" by someone of standing in their community. As approved social workers (responsible for gauging whether a person's liberty should be curtailed because they were a risk to themselves or others) we actively supported those involved to take steps to reverse this, otherwise he or she literally gave up the will to live and obligingly died.

Translating this to the world of cancer treatment, I strongly suspect that the consultant's bad-fairy impersonation was closer to spell casting than we tend to associate with the hi-tech resources he explicitly wields. Clearly an area that needs a lot more attention because myriad other accounts highlight that I am far from being alone in being traumatised by such exchanges.

Not surprisingly it is getting easier now to recognise when I've hit rock bottom which means that I waste less time battling to deny or bargain it out of existence. Bizarrely there might even be something cathartic in the desolation of abject self-pity, when I am forced to acknowledge that my own resources are inadequate and I have no idea how to drag my sorry self through another day. It is one thing to experience wonder at nature's creations when the sun is shining and all is well with the world, quite another to

find a spiritual wholeness which encompasses suffering ... even when I am angry, depressed, tired or spiritually cold. [Advices & Queries # 1.10].

Maybe this is a lesson in humility after a lifetime chasing professional ambitions at the cost of compassion fatigue? Definitely an exercise in trust that there are forces at work that give purpose to both the highs and lows each new day brings.

And then bizarrely – BLISS – the peace that comes from not just rolling over and giving up, but as Mary Lou Leavitt advised in Chapter 1, of letting go and getting out of the way.

Although I have never heard the precise words that Elizabeth Gilbert recorded in the midst of her anguish, the effect resonates most profoundly:

I'm here. I love you. I don't care if you need to stay up crying all night long, I will stay with you. If you need the medication again, go ahead and take it – I will love you through that, as well. If you don't need the medication, I will love you, too. There's nothing you can ever do to lose my love. I will protect you until you die, and after your death I will still protect you. I am stronger than Depression and I am braver than Loneliness and nothing will ever exhaust me.
You're safe now. There is nothing to fear
Trust that when you call I will always answer
And that I have only your best interests at heart
I'm here. I love you
      ("Eat, Pray, Love" Elizabeth Gilbert).

Sometimes the storm abates for no apparent reason, at other times someone or something intercedes.

Energy healing

The most profound experiences of this have come to me during my weekly **Remote healing** sessions – something I would have dismissed as "too wacky" until driven by desperation at the diagnosis to leave no stone unturned. It seems simply too unlikely that I can phone someone 200 miles away and connect with them in such a way that with the briefest exchange of words I can experience profoundly uplifting change. But this has happened reliably over the months!

I have no language to express the truly remarkable sense of being "safe": despite the pain, despite the fears about loss of dignity, despite the despair at watching R endure the unendurable. It is truly a place where all this distress can be laid down and I can return to the thing that underpins everything – the instinctive truth that confirms that I am loved and lovable.

This has had astounding knock on effects - not in terms of providing a magic bullet, which would be to miss the point because as described earlier "healing" is actually about restoring harmony and flow when our physical, mental and emotional bodies have become stuck out of balance. Better than this illusory "cure all", it produces a tangible sensation of being bathed in an energy that revitalises at the deepest cellular level to restore my battered soul. The fact that my ability to manage pain and stress levels (especially in the previous episodes of early morning waking) improves exponentially after these sessions is an unlooked for benefit. Literally transformative - an outwardly dire situation of decline and grief morphs into ongoing opportunities for personal growth. Embarrassing to write about, but nonetheless profoundly true!

Australian bush flower essences

Although I have been blessed that my training and subsequent experiences in social work and as a homeopath have encouraged me to befriend the skeletons in my own wardrobe, I suspect that no-one can be immune to the all-to-human tendency to run away from suffering, constantly burying our pain ever-deeper. In my case it has taken the Australian Bush Flower Essences to reach and discharge the intensity of distress that I could not even have named before encountering descriptions of the range of their actions.

As the name suggests, these (like Bach Flower remedies in UK) are made from the distilled essences of flora indigenous to the region and, rightly or wrongly, they feel to me to have the raw intensity that comes from growing in one of the most inhospitable regions on earth that makes them well-placed to address the profoundly destructive energy of cancer. I have tried to avoid wasting valuable energy on wondering "why me", but feel that there is merit to unravelling the threads in terms of genetic predisposition, lifestyle, illnesses and trauma that have combined through my life to produce this particular susceptibility.

Spinifex

Physical ailments (fine cuts); sense of being a victim to illness

empowerment through emotional understanding; physical healing

I am now seeing the nature and effect of my deeper emotions. Increasingly, I am understanding the emotional causes of my physical problems.

Dagger hakea

Resentment; bitterness

Forgiveness; open expression of feelings

*I am now able to express my feelings
honestly and openly.*

*I now release all buried resentment and
bitterness and am learning to forgive.*

Sturt desert pea

Pain; deep hurt; sadness

Letting go; diffuses sad memories;
motivates + re-energises

*I now release the pain in my past,
I am now able to express my feelings of
sadness and grief.*

For me, the impact of taking a few drops of the essence, several times a day and repeated as required, was increased exponentially by repeating the associated affirmation. As if I was taking responsibility at the deepest level of my being for switching from the negative manifestation of my life's cumulative experiences, to asserting the positive potential of those circumstances.

Just as explored earlier when recognising that our sense

of stress relates not the event but rather than our reaction to it, I discovered with the Australian bush flower essences that they enabled me to simply re-write the programme that involved me carrying long-redundant burdens and strip away the toxicity that had taken root at all levels that had been draining and distorting the expression of my life force.

In the past I have used a wide variety of other complementary therapies that are geared to rebalancing our chakras (energy centres), from crystals, singing bowls to reflexology – all of which proved equally effective in that place and time. It was only at this point in my health journey that I felt drawn to these specific essences, so I have outlined in the Appendix a range of these to enable "newcomers" to alternative health approaches to intuit what would best match their circumstances.

* * * * *

Anam cara

According to Celtic tradition there is an honoured role, known as *Anam Cara*, that translates as 'soul friend', the person whose inner wisdom recognises that they cannot take on our burdens, but rejoices with us knowing the miracle that is represented by the transition we are facing

.. a person you trust enough to share some of the deepest matters of your heart with them, someone who will listen to what you share, without any kind of judgement, without trying to 'fix' anything and without either flattering or criticising you ... like midwives ... assist at the birth ... but don't second guess what form the 'baby' will take ... not there to take the pain away, but to help you deal with it

Margaret Silf *Faith* 2011 Darton,
Longman & Todd Ltd p.53

Different people play this part for me at different times according to their skills, but just as much, their availability – which feels right because then no-one risks being overwhelmed by the task of being truly present during such an emotionally charged time.

So the friend stopping over in the UK en route from her home in Melbourne to visit family in Texas, who had much greater calls on her energy yet arrived with a pack of goodies and most importantly, the commitment to spend 24hours bolstering us up *listening lovingly to whatever we shared ... reflecting back what seemed to be stirring us most deeply ... also challenging us in firm but gentle ways ... warning us if it appeared we were being untrue to our deepest longings and intentions.*

Another sends exquisite packages from India containing imaginative array of delights: essential oils; handmade pouches of cards each with a "thought for the day" to simultaneously provoke and uplift; soaps; batik or block-printed wraps and innumerable traditionally crafted trinkets. The love that has gone into each selection is tangible but the greatest gift of all is the conscious connection that she draws on that transcends the outward differences in our daily lives, to speak to us at a soul level. Like the amethyst butterfly ring that I'm wearing as inspiration whilst writing this section, symbolises so many aspects of my life at this point.

It is neither the size nor cost entailed but rather the shared belief in serendipity – that picking up the phone at this particular moment, forwarding a jokey caption, pulling a book in passing from a shelf, sending a prayer "for no apparent reason".

For all of this generosity and more – my heartfelt gratitude!

Anam Aire

I find that my soul is also yearning increasingly for a style of end-of-life care in which a Cadfael figure and assorted acolytes glide reverentially across courtyards fringed with sun-dappled leaves. Where we, the dying, are comforted as much by birdsong as soft music; our rooms fresh with the fragrance of summer fields just as we are massaged with sweetly scented oils; and all the while held in a state of prayerful trust that diffuses both fear and pain. Such a setting, characterised by contemplation and serenity that enables this period of transition to be enfolded in love, requires a second type of soul companion, known in Celtic as *Anam- Aire*. This 'soul carer' is familiar with the stages we pass through as we shift worlds and can use their wisdom and knowledge to guide us towards achieving the gentle death our soul craves.

In *A safe journey home – a simple guide to achieving a peaceful death,* Felicity Warner identifies some of the gifts that the "soul midwives" she trains seek to provide at the end stage of life:

- *meet your friend 'where they are at' rather than where you'd like them to be*
- *resist the urge to fix, or rescue, or impose your own beliefs*
- *help them find their own source of peace and strength*

- *listen and share, but be silent if that is what is required*
- *help them to cultivate a big perspective and see the long view*
- *have a non-judgemental attitude – encourage your friend to find and express his or her own meaning of life*
- *honour and support their ideas, attitudes and memories*

Most of all she emphasises that by showing true compassion and love, an atmosphere of trust and peace is created

> *... that supports and inspires, which at the deepest level helps the dying to heal themselves spiritually.*

Against all the odds it is this that we witnessed on a frantically busy inner city hospital ward, when R's father was only a few hours away from joining his wife who had died three weeks earlier. Although each bedside was cluttered with banks of monitors that flashed and bleeped, his gathered family created an oasis of calm around him, simply by being united in their love for him and confident that his passing was timely.

The most astounding gift that they received in turn however was that for someone who had chosen to hide from the demands of family life by employing selective deafness, finally joined in fully with the laughter and reminiscing around his bed; even though his hearing aid (and false teeth) had been lost during his admission. No-one present was surprised by his insistence that another chair be fetched to "let your mum sit down"; nor that he then talked openly to this empty chair where he insisted she told him to "stop hanging about being a burden on 'the children'!"

This was an entirely different experience to my mum's death even though she was being cared for in the familiarity of her own home. What featured here was the extent of the denial: family taking turns in playing court jester, avoiding intimacy by being remorselessly upbeat and she in turn regally accepting gifts of fruit and chocolates that she could no longer swallow. With only a few months notice, she and my father never had chance to come to terms with the sense of being robbed of their planned retirement; but did at least re-write their 40 years of marriage into an account that highlighted their strengths as a partnership, censoring the loneliness and isolation of their particular brand of coupledom.

It was hardly surprising then that my sister and I were deeply affected by their combined "soul pain".

> As well as physical pain, most of us are affected by deeper scars, or soul wounds, which don't respond to morphine or sedatives. They exist deep inside, within the dark shadow areas of the psyche, and they hurt

when we least expect them to. They hold us back and stop us from opening ourselves fully to the experience of letting go and surrendering.

* * * *

Conclusion

So, to answer the question,

if from an holistic perspective, to be "healthy" means that our mental, emotional, spiritual and physical energies are balanced – how would we recognise this?

The simple answer is that we judge by outcomes: that I/we become better versions of ourselves.

In my case "healing" is not directed at removing the tumour, because I genuinely believe (though I am sure many others would dismiss it as a "cop out") that none of us know what purpose the challenges we face have in terms of the lessons we, and those around us, need to learn in this lifetime. Instead it is to ensure that through it all my "best self" is brought to the fore, so that whatever lies ahead is encountered with the grace and serenity that comes from the knowledge that it is in keeping with the best interests of my "higher" self/soul purpose (language is SO limiting!).

This simple realisation opens up limitless possibilities in terms of redirecting our energy and efforts to what fundamentally will make a difference to our general health and well-being. But only if we are prepared in turn to embrace a different mind-set and consider its implications, because *with great power, comes great responsibility.* Once we have this awareness we can no longer bumble though life abdicating responsibility … whether for our own health or for the impact of our life choices on the rest of creation.

The crux of the matter seems to be that through the choices we make that inform our behaviour during our lifetime, we each have the opportunity to identify and refine the core values that provide it with a sense of underlying meaning and hence purpose. Then, wherever there is "congruence" between our actions and these values, this creates an integrity that nourishes our Higher self. The premise throughout these musings being that it is these spiritual drives that provide us with the resources to manage the inevitable changes that we encounter along the way fearlessly, in order to transform ourselves into better, happier people even, or particularly when, faced with the prospect of our imminent death.

Fundamental to this is the type of mystical communion that I'm convinced is far more prevalent than we realise – partly because (as Peter and Elizabeth Fenwick recorded in their NDE research *The Truth in the light*) we generally don't have the language to express intangibles; but mainly due to significant under-reporting because of active discouragement in a society that treats spirituality as "spooky" and its proponents as "wacky". Even more suspect than the "navel gazing" of psychotherapy!

In fact, it goes SO much further - confirming too that there is clearly so much more to our world than we can measure with all our state of the art machines. Proof that we optimise our well-being when we live true to ourselves: accessing the still point that allows us to discern what and when opportunities are opening to us

Better still, from everything described above it is clearly not restricted to a certain few "mystics", nor to life and death crises; but is instead always available to us IF we know how to create the appropriate conditions. Just as the person acting as a conduit for my remote healing has a "formula" for achieving the connection between us, by which she can "read" and then connect with universal forces to support the rebalancing of my energies.

We may balk at the idea of "spiritual discipline", assuming that it entails the mind numbing boredom of the school punishment of writing a hundred lines *"I will not ..."*; but even in the west we employ some of its strategies instinctively. We may not be aware for instance as we revel in the sensuality of sinking our hands into the warm, soapy water and allow ourselves albeit briefly to be entranced by the rainbows of light captured in each bubble, that we are achieving a state of mindfulness. We are totally in the present, rather than fretting about past mistakes or future challenges. So it's only a small step to bring these strategies to conscious awareness and therefore being able to reap their rewards, building the equivalent of muscle strength when such exercises are practised regularly.

*   *   *   *

Back in the seventeenth century when George Fox established the Religious Society of Friends (Quakers), it retained its Christian-based tenets, but today membership is drawn from all faiths and none. This fits seamlessly

The common denominator is that we seek to make a direct connection with a force bigger and beyond ourselves, whether we name this specifically as God, the Divine, Spirit or just accept that the concept transcends words and recognise it as a mystical communion with an energy that inspires us to become our best selves. We have no priests or equivalent, but rather worship in silence (unless a Friend is led to "minister") and certainly without hymns or prayers. Instead we wait in the expectation that we will be shown the paths that are opening ahead of us and be made aware of the roles we can play for the enrichment of ourselves and others.

*   *   *   *

Part V: Action Planning

WRAP (Wellness, Recovery Action Planning) is a tool I found on the web and it can be useful for anyone. The site address is: https://www.combined.nhs.uk/person-centredness-framework/wellness-recovery-action-plans-wrap%E2%80%8B/

Wellness Recovery Action Plans (WRAP)

Wellness Recovery Action Plan (WRAP) was created by Mary Ellen Copeland, an author, educator and mental health recovery advocate in the USA.

"WRAP is a tool that can aid an individual's recovery and its underpinning principles support the recovery approach. WRAP is a way of monitoring wellness, times of being less well and times when experiences are uncomfortable and distressing. It also includes details of how an individual would like others to support them at these different times."

WRAP has five key principles:

1. Hope: people who experience mental health difficulties get well, stay well and go on to meet their life dreams and goals.

2. Personal responsibility: it's up to you, with the assistance of others, to take action and do what needs to be done to keep yourself well.

3. Education: learning all you can about what you are experiencing so you can make good decisions about all aspects of your life.

4. Self advocacy: effectively reaching out to others so that you can get what it is that you need, want and deserve to support your wellness and recovery.

5. Support: while working toward your wellness is up to you, receiving support from others, and giving support to others, will help you feel better and enhance the quality of your life.

This is a tool that can be used by anyone who wants to create a positive change in the way they feel and their experience of life. Using it can help us in our recovery journeys of personal discovery. It can help us to live well and to deal with the distress, vulnerabilities and challenges that we all face in our lives.

Benefits:

- it is easy to use, combines common-sense and experience and can therefore be adapted to meet our ever-changing circumstances
- it stresses how we all go through similar processes – but in individual ways, so provides a mix and match approach as situations evolve
- it moves us from being managed to self-management, so can be shared with family, friends carers or remain private

My "toolbox" of things to do to help myself stay well or feel better when emotionally fragile:

1. I have a daily maintenance plan because building up **resilience** to life's events means self knowledge of protective v. predisposing factors i.e. my strengths and what undermines these.

I do this by identifying the things I need to do every day to maintain wellbeing.

To do this start by describing yourself when you're feeling well.

Next identify how you are physically. Ask yourself what level of ability do you have today and what energy is available to you to perform your tasks?

How are you feeling emotionally, are you moody and what level of motivation do you have?

How are you mentally? How's your memory and level of concentration?

Then consider how you are spiritually or creatively.

Therefore by doing

a ....

b ....

c ....

d etc ....

I can take responsibility for my well-being and feel empowered to live to my full potential

2. Triggers – I try to identify the external events / circumstances that, if they happen, can make me feel distressed - giving me the opportunity to avoid them, change them where possible or change the thoughts I am having about them.

3. When things are breaking down – in spite of my best efforts my distress may progress to become very uncomfortable, serious and even dangerous. BUT I can still take action on my own behalf and this is my plan to help me reduce distress (I am directive, provide fewer choices and give very clear instructions to myself)

4. Crisis planning – written when I am well, these are instructions for friends, family members and carers about how to take care of me when I am not well

5. Post crisis planning – what I have learned + therefore can use to avoid or reduce the impact of further episodes

Chapter 5: Cleared for take off

Even if, as in my case, we fall short of achieving the three score years and ten that we have somehow learned we rightfully deserve; I like to think that death will only come when we have achieved all that we can and need from this lifetime? And if for that life span our individual gifts contribute to the well-being of creation we are therefore called on to be nothing more or less than true to ourselves. No more striving after mirages and an end to falling short when I compare myself with others! But it requires a different kind of effort to discern the way forward without being thrown off course by various distractions – so equally demanding.

Chris died before she was able to complete this chapter which remains in note form.

Life purpose – recognising our own gifts

Draw people into our lives who, in the process of pursuing their own path, jointly help us create experiences that provide both parties with the opportunity to learn the lessons this lifetime offers → just as the most painful experiences actually seem, in hindsight to have provided us with the most benefit, so the most challenging relationships have the potential to enable us to achieve our soul's purpose.

Always have options: choice to buy into different "stories" regarding the same event (Q retelling of fairy stories → recasting "villain") means that we can play victim in its many guises and allow ourselves to buy into the illusion that we have had no control over events → toxicity of bitterness, resentment and rage OR accept that we are co-creators of our reality

> *Our complicity in world making is a source of awesome and sometimes painful responsibility - and a source of profound hope for change. It is the ground of our common call to leadership, the truth that makes leaders of us all*
> (*Let your life speak – Listening for the voice of vocation* [2000] Parker J Palmer)

To achieve the latter is to resist the beguiling belief system that encourages us to believe that we are not even cogs in a wheel (interconnected / mutually dependent / of equal value) but (Shakespeare quote – playthings of the gods ...)

> *Optimism is a political act: Entrenched interests use despair, confusion and apathy to prevent change. They encourage modes of thinking which lead us to believe*

that problems are insolvable, that nothing we do can matter, that the issue is too complex to present even the opportunity for change. It is a long-standing political art to sow the seeds of mistrust between those you would rule over: as Machiavelli said, tyrants do not care if they are hated, so long as those under them do not love one another. Cynicism is often seen as an attitude exactly most likely to conform to the desires of the powerful – cynicism is obedience.

Optimism, by contrast, especially optimism which is neither foolish nor silent, can be revolutionary. Where no one believes in a better future, despair is a logical choice, and people in despair almost never change anything. Where no one believes a better solution is possible, those benefiting from the continuation of a problem are safe. Where no one believes in the possibility of action, apathy becomes an insurmountable obstacle to reform. But introduce intelligent reasons for believing that action is possible, that better solutions are available, and that a better future can be built, and you unleash the power of people to act out of their highest principles. Shared belief in a better future is the strongest glue there is: it creates the opportunity for us to love one another, and love is an explosive force in politics. Great movements for social change always begin with statements of great optimism.

[Steffen, A. World changing: a user's guide for the 21st century 2008]

The theme he explores is:

Is the life that I am living the same as the life that wants to live in me?

Issues:

1. *"Vocation"* – from the Latin for voice
ie *not a goal that I pursue. It means a calling that I hear. Before I can tell my life what I want to do with it, I must listen to my life telling me who I am. I must listen for the truths and values at the heart of my own identity, not the standards by which I* **must** *live – but the standards by which I cannot help but live if I am living my own life*

2. "Leadership" is often a concept we resist. It seems immodest, even self-aggrandizing, to think of ourselves as leader. But if it is true that we are made for community, then leadership is everyone's vocation, and it can be an evasion to insist that it is not. When we live in the close-knit ecosystem called community, everyone follows and everyone leads

... I have come to understand that for better or for worse, I lead by word and deed **simply because I am here doing what I do**. *If you are also here, doing what you do, then you also exercise leadership of some sort.*

He suggests that there are 5 "shadows" that obstruct our own spiritual authenticity and hence our ability to contribute our gifts fully to the benefit of ourselves and the different communities to which we belong:

* insecurity about identity and worth – rather than grounded in the knowledge that identity does not depend on the role we play or the power it gives us over others → confident that as children of God we are all valued in and for ourselves, our actions are life affirming

* the belief that the universe is a battle ground, hostile to human interests risks becoming a self-fulfilling prophesy whereas creating a different "reality" of consensual + co-operative community reveals the spiritual truth that harmony is fundamental in nature → we can learn to move gracefully with that cycle and in doing so transform the nature of our institutions / way of living + doing business

* "functional atheism" – the belief that ultimate responsibility (particularly if anything good is going to happen, but also for "failure") rests with us – whereas when we learn to share "the load" we liberate ourselves + empower others. *The great community asks us only to do what we are able and trust the rest to other hands"*

* fear – especially fear of the natural chaos of life, instead of seeing the positives of "messiness" ie dissent, innovation,

challenge + change. Because chaos is the precondition for creativity

* the denial of death - rather than recognising our connectedness with the natural cycles of life, where death of the old makes way for renewal / regeneration in a more vital form. Therefore leaps of faith are worthwhile because the death of one initiative / structure is always the source of new learning

Conclusion

We are not the victims of society, but its co-creators … (so if we) find ourselves confined, it is only because we have conspired in our own imprisonment … by projecting our spirit on it, for better or for worse. If our institutions are rigid, it is because our hearts fear change; if they set us in mindless competition with each other, it is because we value victory over all else; if they are heedless of human well-being, it is because something in us is heartless as well. We can make choices about what we are going to project, and with those choices we help grow the world that is i.e. each individual's **Consciousness** can form, deform or reform our world

> Without a global revolution in the sphere of human consciousness, nothing will change for the better …and the catastrophe toward which this word is headed, whether it be

ecological, social, demographic or a general breakdown of
civilisation, will be unavoidable

(*The Art of the Impossible* - speech to US Congress 1997 Vaclav Havel president of Czech republic)

Human Givens (Griffin J. & Tyrrell I. 2003 p 93-4)

Human emotional needs include:

- Security – safe territory + environment
- Attention – to give + receive it
- Sense of autonomy + control
- Being emotionally connected to others
- Belonging – part of a wider community
- Friendship + intimacy
- Sense of status
- Sense of competence + achievement
- Sense of meaning + purpose

The resources nature gave us to help us meet those needs include:

- The ability to build rapport, empathise + connect with others

- Imagination that helps us focus attention AWAY from our emotions → problem solve more creatively + effectively
- A conscious, rational mind that can check out emotions, question, analyse + plan (brain's left hemisphere)
- The ability to "know" – understand the world unconsciously through metaphorical pattern-matching (brain's right hemisphere)
- An observing self that can step back and be more objective (frontal lobes)

→ *Joy + Laughter*

Five Love Languages   (Gary Chapman)

i. Words of Affirmation:

verbal compliments

words of appreciation / encouragement / kindness

positive remarks

praising to a 3rd party will get back to the subject of the praise!

(avoid nagging, subtle hints, sarcasm, humiliation, criticism)

Ideas:

- Set a goal to pay a different compliment each day
- Listen out for (and keep a list of?) positive remarks used by others
- Praise someone in front of others
- Make a point of commenting on people's strengths
- Write thank you notes

ii. Quality Time – sharing undivided attention during eg meals, activities, trips etc

* give focussed attention via "active listening" – maintaining eye contact, reflecting back, clarifying, mirroring → seeking the meaning "behind" the words

* stop what you're doing in order to go to welcome someone after their absence, assist in carrying bags, offer refreshments etc

* display empathy → genuine desire to learn more about hopes/ fears not defensive

* avoid interrupting / interjecting your own "solutions", opinions, advice etc

* pay attention to body language (especially where it is different from the words being expressed)

* share experiences, thoughts, feelings, desires in a friendly, uninterrupted context

* prioritise regular "dates" and share responsibility for taking the initiative in arranging surprises

* allow room for spontaneity and "being" together companionably rather than always "doing" – turn "chores" like grocery shopping into shared fun eg by taking a detour through the park to feed the ducks

* be willing to try new experiences + be positive when embarking on an activity, even if you don't share the same passions!

* be open to learning more about yourself through these exchanges + communicate these insights → shared intimacy via emotional disclosure / self revelation

Ideas:

- Be as attentive as if you're dating: hold hands whilst you walk + talk, encourage each other to play / be creative + rediscover spontaneity / fun
- Develop emotional literacy ie recognising the specific feelings triggered by different events and

practice talking about these until you feel comfortable "owning" even the "negative" emotions

- Recognise your communication style – preferring or avoiding silence (AKA "good listener" / "vivacious companion"; introvert / extravert) and learn when to play to your strengths or meet ½ way
- Record the experiences for memory / nostalgia-fests!
- Beware of letting the daily routine / work demands sap your commitment to spending the quality time required to nourish your relationships – instead foster a sense of embarking on a never ending voyage of discovery

iii. Giving - Receiving Gifts – visual symbols of love irrespective of cost because love underlines the spirit in which the gift is given, intimate knowledge about what the recipient likes / appreciates and shared meaning eg metaphor for life together

Ideas:

- Discover the value of "handmade" originals + / or gifts from nature eg shells, feathers, flowers in season
- Keep a gift list where you keep a note of the things that give the recipient pleasure, present

attractively and include a gift tag with a heartfelt sentiment

- Don't restrict yourself to special occasions or costly items – giving an suitable article from a magazine demonstrates your support of their ideas /aspirations
- Give a lasting tribute – eg to charity / plant a tree – as a lasting honour for the recipient

iv. Acts of Service – because "little things" literally do "mean a lot"

* putting the thought, planning, time, effort + energy into "doing" all the tasks that keep life ticking over, with a positive spirit – even if this means challenging stereotypes about traditional male / female roles

* physical presence in the time of crisis

* setting boundaries to discourage manipulation, being taken for granted   **Love says "I love you too much to let you treat me this way – it isn't good for you or me!"**

Ideas:

- Pay attention not only to the requests being made for assistance, but also their priority so that you can commit to responding, even if there may be a time delay

- Enlist a team of helpers to complete a difficult task as a surprise
- Tagging not nagging – redefine any repetition of requests as clues to the priority placed by the other person on a particular action, so completing these as an expression of love is worth more than any token gift
- Give praise / show sincere appreciation for effort
- Attach a gift tag to eg the car that has been cleaned, handle of a room tidied with " To ... from ... with love"

v. Physical Touch – research has shown that babies who are held, hugged + kissed develop a healthier emotional life, but as we get older we increasingly confuse touch and sexuality, so many adults are literally "touch starved"

* Not all touches give pleasure, so check out that the recipient is able to welcome rather than rebuff the contact (eg not up to their elbows in washing dishes!)

* Share responsibility for initiating physical contact so that the risk of rejection is also shared

* Non-sexual touch such as shoulder massage demonstrates that you not only recognise, but want to relieve their physical + / or emotional tension

* Physical comfort is often much more appropriate than words during a crisis, because being able to hold someone when they are crying demonstrates that you are willing to share their distress without trying to "fix" it

Ideas

- Increase opportunities for incidental touches to reinforce a sense of mutual comfort rather than always as a precursor to sex
- Check "no-go" areas before assuming that everyone enjoys the same level of contact – eg for many the vogue for 2 cheek kissing seems phony or overly intimate, whereas good eye contact + smile conveys greater sincerity
-

A Safe Journey Home – A Simple Guide to Achieving a Peaceful Death – *Felicity Warner.*

Growing spiritually – embracing difference
Myers Briggs
Forgiveness and reconciliation - conflict resolution

Fruits of the Spirit - *the greatest of which is Love* (Corinths)

Chapter 6: Post Script

This started to take form early in the new year of 2016 when any premonitions of death for instance were entirely at odds with how robust I looked. So I needed it as an outlet, because in a society geared to rewarding youth and productivity, taking ourselves (and therefore heaven forbid our health) too seriously, is actively discouraged. In fact, throughout the previous autumn it had been relatively easy to over-ride any warning signs by viewing developments as simply a reaction to turning 60 in May. But despite the "what do you expect at your age?" default response, deep down I knew that that there is no automatic link between years chalked up and exponential increases in frailty.

Not even really a journal, it has therefore acted as a release valve to discharge the hamster wheeling thoughts that drove my early morning waking, which had in turn been prompted by a series of earlier health scares. A safe way to contain the nagging doubts resulting from the constant battle against an exhaustion that was way out of proportion even with the stresses of being self-employed during a decade long recession. For me there was no way that *"60 is the new 40!"*

Fortunately, I'm not a stranger to the hinterlands: after all, I'd qualified as a social worker in Lambeth in the riots of the mid 80's, when the catchy slogan "*Save a London child, kill a social worker*" reflected the media's scapegoating of a profession trying to stem the rising inequalities of the Thatcher era. Then, having discovered complementary therapies as the only effective approach to treating the M.E type symptoms that I had developed after exposure to illegal crop spraying of organophosphates; I retook all the science GCSE's and A levels that I had failed so spectacularly the first time round, only to swap from studying nutritional sciences to a 4 year course in homeopathy.

Moving from "wet liberal" to "snake oil peddler" and "charlatan" in the process, I then started to discover piecemeal the facts that have since become common knowledge. Not least the stranglehold that *Big Pharma* and the multi-national food corporations have had in undermining the health and well-being of the population of an entire planet!

Not only is being unpopular professionally a great spur to independent thinking, so the realisation that there are others who are like-minded has been invaluable in providing validation when I'm questioning my motives and insecure about outcomes.

Amongst Quakers, who have five testimonies to Simplicity, Truth, Equality, Peace and Sustainability, and with them I've discovered a language to formulate my spirituality in ways that go far beyond what is offered by more orthodox religions. Excerpts from 'Quaker Faith and Practice' published by Britain Yearly Meeting have proved invaluable in supplying the scaffolding for these musings.

Most recently I've made contact with the fast growing community of those inspired by being or working with the terminally ill. This has shown me that I'm far from alone in exploring what it means to achieve a "good death" and given me the confidence to ask the $1m question: might this be achievable if Nature is largely allowed to take its course rather than have health crises mismanaged by medical interventions that can only buy time rather than extend quality of life?

So, if this is to be my swan song, I'd like it to be a rung on the ladder for those who, like me, have unwittingly spent time reinventing the wheel instead of being able to tap into existing resources to challenge the fear-driven myths about death. If, in so doing, it helps us fully appreciate the miracle of who we are, by unpicking the link with the western medical model's focus on pathology and the overload of misinformation that we are force fed through the media by those whose vested interests are diametrically opposite to sustaining health; so much the better!

There are however great chunks of the work that I feel I can take little credit for: it is as if something outside myself has translated essentially mundane musings into a coherent whole. This is particularly true of the format that has emerged, with the comparison of undertaking a long-haul flight. It evolved from the realisation that, after we've removed the drama from the equation, preparing to die involves going through a series of essentially predictable stages that are parallel to those of any journey we make.

It's just that managing this dying is not the equivalent of arranging a cheap weekend jolly - more like planning a major expedition, involving a rigorous training regimen (psychological as much as physical), with as much behind-the-scenes activity by an experienced support team. I base this conclusion on talk-show interviews I've seen with adventurers talking about the success or otherwise of their expeditions: where they invariably describe the years of planning, but above all cite psychological discipline as the key ingredient.

Anything as important as our dying therefore should surely not be left to fate wherever possible? If there is a vast array of resources from which to pick and mix, I'd like to think that it is possible to customise them, so that in keeping with our own circumstances and aptitudes,

each of us can prepare a bespoke programme that
ensures we thrive rather than simply survive in the time
remaining to us?

Back in time

Familiarity with death came with the territory in a mining
community. This was still the case even in the late 50's,
though by this time the nationalisation of the coal
industry had replaced the more gung-ho attitudes that
the private mining companies had to worker safety and
welfare. It only meant however that the living-death of
pneumoconiosis, "miner's lung", replaced pit accidents as
the most likely end to a lifetime's work. Within my own
family it was said to be the impact of digging his part-
baked colleagues out after the Sneyd pit disaster, which
triggered the cancer that widowed my grandmother,
leaving her with 7 school aged children to somehow feed.

And then there was Aberfan ... where a primary school's
pupils were buried alive when the slag heap of mining
waste that had grown like a pyramid alongside the
winding gear, avalanched into the valley. My Dad was
part of the investigating team and so returned home to
his own 2 daughters, also in primary school, but in this
case living beneath the shadow of Whitfield colliery's slag
heap, now towering malevolently above the village. If
he'd been religious, he's have said "there but for the

Grace of God", but such senseless loss makes for unbelievers.

Closer to home, I must have been about 4 years old when I stood with my 18month old sister and father, in the bright sunshine, amidst graves swathed in daffodils; as my Mum joined her 5 sisters burying their own father. The suddenness of a heart attack left them reeling. But my grandfather's first wife had died from the Spanish flu whilst nursing wounded soldiers; my grandmother's fiancée had been killed in action, leaving her with the prospect of raising their child "out of wedlock". So when the two married they already had a family of 3 daughters. Then the much-longed for son died at birth, strangled by his umbilical cord ...

So death was as much a part of every family's life as birth: even recognised in the same way, with the rattle of the poker on the back of the grate that separated the terraced houses, to alert neighbours, as it frequently seemed, to "one in, one out". I grew up familiar with the photos of preternaturally young uncles who had been killed in the desert, or later, cousins who had died in motor bike accidents. I must also have attended wakes where the body, dressed in Sunday best, was laid out in the parlour for several days of goodbyes. There would have been hushed voices, but also drinking, laughter and singing – as well as a fair few rows as the scabs of long-festering resentments were picked over! Death was nothing more or less eventful than family Christmases or weddings, simply another set of rituals binding together an ever-changing landscape of relationships.

As a tomboy, intimations of my own mortality also arrived early, with various dramatic falls invariably involving stitches and even surgery. As the years passed, many more "near misses" were attributed by the adults involved to my being accident prone. In fact I've subsequently recognised them as the result of "out of body" episodes and faced the associated challenge of learning how to stay conscious of the physical limitations of gangly arms and legs. Set this however in the context of aunts who disappeared for a few months after their behaviour had become increasingly distressed (read "distressing to those around") and then were "never themselves" when they just as mysteriously reappeared. It was made perfectly clear that the rules were unbreakable, "if you can't touch it, it doesn't exist".

So the rest of my life has been an exploration of what else is out there. Why could I see a sheath, like cling-film, skewing my Nan's body, which I simultaneously wanted to and yet feared to, peel back in order to free her limbs from the paralysis caused by her stroke? How could I, as a remarkably young child, have access to knowledge that the adults refused adamantly to even countenance. It was the "*Emperor's new clothes*" without the feel-good conclusion of the shared Eurika moment. Instead, there were the put down's of "you think too much … stop making trouble … who do you think you are" and the most dire threat of all - "it'll end in tears!" (with the implicit "and they'll be yours!").

So death became un-talked of yet as prevalent as birth.

These then are my musing on the subject, based on my experiences and knowledge gained. If there is just one line in this book or one idea which helps you or those around you manage dying better then, I am happy.

Chris wanted a kindred spirit to be with her while she died.

Chris was diagnosed with a life limiting cancer on 22nd January 2016 and was given the prognosis of one year. Over three years later, she was admitted to the hospice in October 2019 as the pain she was experiencing had significantly increased and we knew the management of pain would be more easily controlled in a hospice setting. Throughout her time in the hospice she was listened to, treated with and maintained her dignity till her death on the 19th December, 2019.

Three days before she died the pain had become unbearable and to my undying gratefulness she was made unconscious. I stayed by her side for those three days, accompanied for much of the time by one of Chris's friends. Other friends came and I hope they were able to say their 'goodbyes'.

On the last day the sun was shining, it was a brisk sun-filled day; a day filled with life. Her breathing had begun to change becoming more laboured and intermittent. The nurses, who had provided us both so much care and consideration, forewarned me of her imminent death.

She stopped breathing after taking, what I took to be a final gulp of air and as I pressed the buzzer for the nurse who responded immediately, she began breathing once more. The nurse gave me a gentle smile, then a reaffirming nod and kindly left us alone together, no doubt knowing from experience this was the end of Chris's time on Earth.

I took hold of Chris's hand and stood close to her looking into her unseeing eyes and remembered what to do. The memory came from the many car journeys we had taken together. Whenever we went on a journey the driver would always sing. Chris always sang her repertoire of George Formby classics while, when it was my turn to drive, I would always sing songs from the musicals.

Well, here we were. Chris was about to go on her greatest journey ever and it looked like I was in the driving seat. So I gently sang to her the love song from Carousel, *'If I loved you'*. As I did, it felt to me as if she was pushing herself upwards and looking upwards towards a place still hidden from me. As I came to the end of the song I saw her eyes lose their colour and felt her spirit leave her body and I knew Chris's Awfully Big Adventure was continuing elsewhere.

I wept then and I weep now, yet she went with all my love and, love is the energy which never dies.

R

Appendix Resources & References

It is impossible to do more than outline the range of safe and natural alternatives available, so use the library for information / books on any of the following subjects that interest you; and look out for free "taster" sessions offered by specific therapists

Aromatherapy:

uses the fragrance in specific oils to promote healing, build confidence and enhance relaxation (can be used with **Massage**)

Body workers: Bowen; Chiropractic; Osteopathy; Physiotherapy, Pilates

after physical injuries that have result in problems with spine, pelvis, limbs etc to help reduce head aches and generally improve pain management. Case studies have also illustrate the wide range of emotional issues that can be relieved by realigning spine + skull – from changes in personality following head injury, to depression etc

Homeopathy:

uses potentised remedies that aid recovery from anxiety / depression – particularly helpful where underlying physical and emotional trauma are fuelling distress

"Mindfullness":

an approach geared to short cutting our tendency to drive ourselves on a hamster wheel, fixating over past or future events, rather than getting respite in the harmony of the present moment. An effective self-help tool (and available on NHS but practitioner skills levels vary widely!)

Nutritional medicine (eg Ayurveda):

Recognises that foods have healing properties:

- helping to control levels of eg blood sugar, hormones etc to stabilise energy levels and mood;
- challenging tendencies to comfort eat or other methods of using food to distract ourselves from emotional distress;
- identifying food intolerances, particularly those that compound behavioural difficulties (eg wheat, dairy, colourings +additives, sugars, processed foods, caffeine)

Visualisation techniques:

are used by many practitioners to "re-programme" the brain when stress and emotions are at a high level; often used alongside **breathing exercises** to aid relaxation reduce stress and improve sleep patterns

PAIN MANAGEMENT

As with most symptoms, pain is the body's way of telling us something is amiss and needs addressing. If we suppress the symptoms with conventional pain killers, or provide symptomatic relief without looking at any underlying causes; there is a danger that the body's natural healing process will be compromised so that acute conditions recur or become chronic. Lasting improvement or effective healing can however be achieved if these factors are identified and addressed

IDENTIFYING the UNDERLYING CAUSE

1. Sleep deprivation has been found to increase levels of pro-inflammatory chemicals by between 40 – 60% and dehydration will result in a build up of toxins that will aggravate symptoms

2. Consider whether excessive weight is a contributory factor

3. Check that posture is good and that exercise is a regular part of everyday activities

4. Dietary factors:

> - some foods and drinks promote inflammation in some people   e.g. sugar, refined flour products, caffeine, dairy, alcohol and anything containing trans fats (such as biscuits and cakes).

> - Leaky gut, candida and parasites can all add to the inflammation load on the body

5. Adrenal, thyroid and sex hormone imbalances can exacerbate pain

6. Has there been exposure to toxic substances (at work, by decorating or using certain household cleaners)? Even beauty products may be implicated especially petrol-based products, hair dye etc

7. People with chronic pain often endure considerable additional distress as a result of their condition: reduced confidence, social isolation, marital and financial problems, fear and depression. Addressing these issues is also fundamental to well-being

8. The Body-Mind connection

- What was going on in your life around the time the pain started – possibly trauma related?
- Do you tend to suppress, ignore or deny your feelings? (This can make the experience of pain greater)
- Are you stressed?

- Are your emotional needs (safety, security, intimacy, meaning, purpose and social connection) being met? Not doing so causes distress, whether or not you can feel it

Disadvantages of treating chronic pain with prescribed or over the counter medications (OTCM)

- Drugs containing codeine and dihydrocodeine are know to be highly addictive. An estimated 30,000 people in the UK are addicted to OTCM

- It was announced in 2005 that co-proxamol, one of the most heavily prescribed paracetemol containing drugs was to be withdrawn over a 2 year period because of its link with suicide. This is only one example of the pharmaceutical companies by-passing safety standards, withholding key data and /or circulating misleading information about their products

- Recent data from a large British study found that non-steroidal anti-inflammatory drugs (NSAIDs) e.g. Ibuprofen, increase the risk of stroke and heart failure and double the risk of heart attacks. Other side-effects include kidney damage, production / exacerbation of asthma-type symptoms, gastrointestinal bleeding and deterioration in mood

- At the time of writing it is estimated that around 25 million prescriptions for NSAIDs are issued in the UK each year, resulting in 12,000 admissions to hospital to treat serious side effects; with as many as 2,000 deaths per year

Homeopathy

Working from an holistic viewpoint means that we believe that our body will always make the best possible adjustment to a given set of circumstances and particularly, that measures will be taken to protect vital organs. As a result we frequently see symptoms of inflammation affecting skin and or joints – painful, but not life threatening. Only if these symptoms are suppressed and the imbalance they represent is denied an outlet, will the condition impact on our other organs e.g. eczema suppressed has been linked with the development of asthma.

Most homeopathic remedies have the ability to reduce inflammation and help with pain management, but particularly:

Arnica for over exertion or being physically / emotionally battered
Rhus-tox +/or **Ruta** for damage to joints and ligaments
Symphytum for bone injuries
Hypericum for damage to nerve rich areas (including the spine)
Bellis-perennis for damage to soft tissue e.g. abdomen, breasts
Nat-sulph after head injuries etc.

It is essential therefore that a detailed case history is taken, because in many instances, the pain is simply the tip of an ice berg and to respond appropriately we need to understand why, when, what, how it arose and ironically perhaps, what function it is performing. Otherwise we run the same risk of missing the underlying problem and only providing short-lived relief.

Top Tips for managing pain naturally

Always discuss with your health professionals and other qualified practitioners before self-treating, to ensure your goals are realistic and sustainable. A 10% reduction in symptoms may not sound much, but the resulting improvement in sleep alone can raise spirits and so produce a significant boost to the quality of life

1. Identify contributory factors then consider

* (cranial) osteopathy, (McTimoney) chiropractic treatment, and/ or pilates; acupuncture, massage / aromatherapy; homeopathy or herbal approaches to redress specific recurring conditions

* addressing any emotional issues that are contributing to your stress levels eg via counselling, Cognitive Behaviour therapy etc

* incorporating visualisations as part of your pain management strategy

2. Aim for a whole food diet with sufficient fibre and 1 - 3L of water to ensure at least one comfortable bowel movement per day

- beware bran if a wheat intolerance is suspected
- psyllium husk capsules can help in the short term and will assist in the healing of the gastro-intestinal tract, but should not be relied on long-term
- replace coffee and tea with white tea, nettle tea or rooibos, which all have anti-inflammatory properties

If food sensitivities and allergies are a possibility, try cutting out 1 main suspect for up to 6 weeks. If you gain relief but reintroducing the item brings on a return of symptoms consider discussing with your GP

3. Consider quality supplements to combat any deficiencies in diet (inevitable if food has been grown intensively, stored for extended periods or otherwise processed) – particularly:

    i.   essential vitamins and minerals, which by definition our bodies cannot produce

    ii.   essential fatty acids (found in oily fish but avoid "farmed" because of pesticide residue; hemp / flax seed oils) – these help reduce inflammation, restore cell integrity, improve functioning of the myelin sheath which transmits nerve impulses

Seek professional advice to ensure "safe" doses and to obtain optimum benefit because:

- bone, joint, muscle or nerves conditions require different approaches
- due to the way they interact, excessive intake of one vitamin / mineral will prevent the absorption of others

4. Adjust your routine so that you have approx 20 minutes in the open air – Vitamin D is obtained most easily from sunlight and plays a key role in calcium assimilation

5. Increase mobility and build in a personalised exercise regime including low-impact activities (e.g. hydrotherapy / water aerobics)

TOP 10 TIPS for Healthy Eating

The following suggestions are changes that can be gradually built in to your lifestyle. This means that they will be more easily maintained in the long-term and certainly should never give you a sense that you are being deprived of your favourite food or pastimes.

1. Eat as wide a variety of fresh produce as possible and prepare simply to avoid the inevitable nutrient loss involved in storing or cooking

2. Include foods from the five main groups: fruit and vegetables; carbohydrates (eg bread, other cereals and potatoes); protein (meat, fish, eggs and alternatives) plus dairy (milk, cream, cheese, yoghurt) and finally small amounts of unsaturated fats / oils

3. A 'portion' of the first 2 groups is roughly the amount of food that fits comfortably into your palm eg for an adult: 3 cherry tomatoes or 3 whole dried apricots, a small bunch of grapes, a medium apple; or the equivalent in cooked / chopped foods eg a cereal bowl of salad, medium glass of fruit juice, 3 heaped tablespoons of peas or beans

4. Aim to eat locally sourced or organic products that contain higher levels of the essential trace elements; checking for minimum use of pesticides, hormones etc. The very fact that these have greater flavour means that our appetite will be more easily satisfied, so we eat less and ultimately save money.

5. Present food attractively, then pay attention to the different taste sensations and chew thoroughly – the digestive process starts when enzymes are secreted at the first sight /smell of food and is enhanced by a relaxed

atmosphere; so avoid eating on the run, at your desk or in front of the TV

6. Build in opportunities to exercise: even 30 minutes a day (eg parking further away from out-of-office appointments, taking a walk during lunch, gardening) has the added benefits of lifting the mood and improving uptake of vitamin D (essential in calcium assimilation)

7. Drink small amounts of quality, still water regularly through the day but limit during meals because it can interfere with the digestive processes. Increase particularly if you are prone to headaches. We also often reach for food when we are in fact dehydrated

8. If you need to take antibiotics, follow with a course of good quality probiotics (not Actimel) available from Bioforce, Higher Nature etc

9. If you suffer from digestive complaints do not mask symptoms with over the counter medication, but view them as your body's alarm call and address the root cause naturally to avoid the risk of side effects. There are even alternatives to diuretics and laxatives that are gentler yet just as effective

10. Most skin symptoms, discharges or fevers are healthy ways of your body fighting infection or eliminating poisons. Herbs and supplements that support specific organs can easily be incorporated into your meals to improve levels of functioning

Miscellaneous:

If you are prone to mood swings or energy crashes during the day beware:

- caffeine – in coffee, tea; "high energy" drinks; many soft drinks; painkillers

- sugars (includes anything ending in –ose) – often hidden in 'low fat' foods to compensate for the flavour lost by removing the fat

- daily alcohol

- over-reliance on products containing wheat / yeast – especially if you have had several courses of antibiotics

The following are also implicated in food intolerances and can aggravate existing allergies:

- hydrogenated and trans fatty acids – anything that makes fat 'spreadable'

- aspartane, monosodium glutamate (MSG) and the raft of additives designed to extend the shelf-life of products and mask 'dodgy' ingredients

Finally:
- the consumption of fizzy drinks has been linked to a higher incidence of bone fractures in youngsters and increases the risk of osteoporosis

- too much salt can lead to high blood pressure and strokes – since salt is present in many of our foods (particularly tinned / processed) strategies for reducing intake include using alternatives such as herbs, spices, vinegars, garlic, lemon juice or ground pepper to enhance flavour. Always taste food before adding salt

HEALTHY EATING STRATEGIES

1. Avoid blood sugar lows by snacking on 1 portion of nuts, seeds, dried or fresh fruit between meals and prioritise items that release energy slowly (eg oats in porridge, oatcakes etc) to avoid the sudden 'highs' of fruit bars, breakfast cereals etc
   For more information Google "low glycaemic index"

2. Keep quality water accessible – it is so much easier to drink the advised 6-8 glasses if it is to hand. Add a squeeze of lemon juice or fresh root ginger for flavour but beware fruit juice because of its high acid and sugar content. The best test of "how much is enough?" is light coloured urine (excluding the first of the day)

3. If feeling under par, choose warm drinks and lightly cooked food because raw food / cold drinks place more demands on the body's energy reserves (but this therefore makes them a good choice if the goal is gradual weight loss)

4. Avoid using food + / or alcohol ("empty calories") to comfort or as a 'treat' – substitute other low cost activities e.g.: an extra 10 minutes reading for

pleasure; taking a relaxing (candle-lit) bath; investing in aromatherapy oils for massage or room fragrance

5. Experiment by adding at least 2 unfamiliar vegetables, fruits, herbs / spices to your weekly shop (preferably seasonal) and find alternative recipes for the regulars

6. Research natural alternatives e.g.:
- ½ tsp of cinnamon daily is said to lower blood pressure
- herbal supplements - cynara to lower cholesterol; crataegus (hawthorn) for circulatory disorders eg atherosclerosis ("furring" of the arteries); dandelion / milk thistle to support liver / detoxification; berberis for kidney + urinary tract

NB 1st seek professional advice if you are on prescribed medication

7. Less is more: substitute fruit for 'sweets' and indulge in small amounts of quality items which are more satisfying / less calorific than multi-saves eg plain chocolate, high (70%+) in cocoa solids can offer many benefits

8. Put simply "fat makes us fat" – this applies as much to "healthy" unsaturated fats, so use with caution. A small amount however (e.g. 25g cheese) taken with fruit will trigger a sense of satisfaction better than fruit alone and omega rich oils (as in oily fish) are essential for cellular repair, nerve function and act to reduce inflammatory conditions

9. It is advisable to have at least one bowel movement daily. Most people can successfully take psyllium husk capsules if either diarrhoea or constipation is a problem, because these provide bulk to slow the transit time and / or a mucous coating to ease elimination. Consider whether stress is contributing to any digestive irregularity (as with Irritable Bowel Syndrome) and implement strategies to redress this

The Facts of Life

Water
Approximately 70% of the human body is water. To be at our best adults therefore need to absorb on average 2.5 Litres of fluid per day, which will be recycled and ultimately lost via urine (1.5L); 700ml(breathing); 200ml (sweat); 100ml (faeces)

Facts:
- we would die faster from lack of water than from starvation

- fizzy drinks may increase the risk of weakened bones - possibly because the body diverts calcium to neutralise the acidity produced by the carbon dioxide "fizz" from its essential role in bone formation or the phosphorous content of the drinks alters the delicate balance of minerals in the body and causes calcium to be broken down. Irrespective of the reason, 1/5th of fizzy drink addicts were found to have suffered fractures before the age of 20

- caffeine (also found in cola and "high energy" drinks, medications e.g. Lemsip) and alcohol, not only deplete the body of essential nutrients but encourage dehydration. (Tea drinkers however have stronger bones than non tea drinkers, which suggests that the fluoride and flavonoids ie plant chemicals that act as anti-oxidants, contained in tea promote bone density – whilst added milk produced even higher bone mineral density, particularly in the hip area!)

Fibre
... the "roughage" that controls the transit time of foods through the digestive system, so that nutrients can be absorbed and toxins eliminated promptly.

Facts:

- processed foods have had much of the natural fibre removed and will therefore release sugars faster into the blood stream, causing dramatic swings in moods as well as energy levels

- whole grains are rich in vitamins, minerals and plant chemicals whereas processed carbohydrates (e.g. white flour and rice) can lose e.g. 98% of chromium, 77% of zinc

- beans and pulses are a major and inexpensive source of complex carbohydrates, protein and essential minerals / fatty acids

Fats
Diets rich in saturated fats (dairy and meat products) contain high levels of LDL (low density lipoproteins ie "bad cholesterol") that can cause the arteries to clog and increase the risk of heart disease. Unsaturated and polyunsaturated fats (oily fish, nuts, seeds and their oils) contain essential fatty acids and HDL (High Density Lipoproteins ie "good cholesterol") that are essential in the formation and functioning of cellular tissues, brain function and vision. They are however high in calories, so should be used sparingly.

Facts:
- polyunsaturated oils as they are easily damaged e.g. by the heat involved in frying so avoid in cooking, though great in mayonnaise or salad dressing

- fats are responsible for imparting flavour – so beware "low fat" foods, because these will be higher in calories due to the extra salt and/or sugar required to make them palatable

- The benefits of eating foods containing Essential Fatty Acids (EFAs also improvement in skin conditions; lowered blood pressure; increased functioning of the nervous and immune systems. Beware oily fish e.g. farmed salmon which contain high levels of pesticides

Nutrients
The food we eat supplies the vitamins and minerals essential for all life's processes (growth, repair and to activate almost all chemical reactions etc) in a natural and well-balanced form that cannot be duplicated as effectively by chemical supplementation

Facts:
There are however several factors that make us more at risk of developing chronic health conditions:
- high levels of pollution mean that a considerable amount of the body's available energy needs to be diverted into detoxification, away from important life-enhancing processes

- intensive farming and food production / preparation methods deplete the levels of nutrients, especially essential minerals (hence the importance of buying / growing organic produce)

- poor quality supplements fail to provide nutrients in forms that can be absorbed by the body e.g. drinks containing probiotics are unlikely to survive transit through stomach acid in order to benefit the digestive tract

- the issue of supplementation is generally oversimplified e.g. taking calcium tablets (i.e. chalk!) to redress osteoporosis will potentially:

- limit the body's ability to absorb its "partner" Phosphorous
- increase the risk of kidney stones
Whereas daily exposure to sunlight (20 minutes) increases the production of retinol and hence Vitamin D which aids the absorption of calcium, which is also available in a wider range of foods other than dairy products

- the concept of "empty calories" ie minimal nutritional value but high in calories, is overlooked by advertisers keen to mobilise children's "pester power" for e.g. breakfast cereals - completely at odds with the Government's stated goal in tackling the "epidemic" of childhood obesity.

- Diets high in red meats create very strong acids that take about 5 days for the body to clear through the kidneys, after neutralising with alkaline minerals e.g. calcium and diverting it from bone formation etc. Such diets are therefore associated with e.g. gout, osteoporosis and urinary infections. Increasing % intake of fruit and vegetables therefore not only exceeds the minimum RDA (recommended daily allowance) of 5 portions (of 80g or equivalent to a palm size) a day, but helps the body fluids remain within the optimum pH range (ie slightly alkaline)

- Eating a diverse diet also reduces over-exposure to common foods that have been linked to adverse health reactions including asthma, eczema, psoriasis and arthritis (worst offenders: wheat, dairy produce, citrus fruits, corn, yeast)

- The colours in plant foods relate to the different phytochemicals they contain, each of which has particular health benefits. Eaten daily in different combinations, they act as anti-oxidants that will "mop up" free radicals (cancer forming cells)

- Many commercially available food items contain a cocktail of additives and preservatives geared to improving appearance, disguising poor quality and extending shelf life. Labelling continues to be misleading and guidance regarding food standards inadequate. Of particular concern is the vulnerability of babies and young children because: the immaturity of their organs (especially kidneys) makes them less capable of dealing with toxins; they have a higher intake of food and water per unit of body weight than adults; their digestive systems are more efficient at absorbing what they eat. Even organic baby-foods have been criticised for containing excessive levels of salt and sugars - see www.annabelkarmel.com for advice + recipes from world expert on baby and child nutrition.

Top tips for Refreshing sleep

Most people need a minimum of 8 hours sleep per night to provide the opportunity for our physical and mental systems to rest, repair and renew themselves. Recent research has shown that losing a mere 1/2hour each night results in reduced academic performance, increased moodiness and even the likelihood of obesity.

- Avoid caffeine (found not only in coffee, but also cola drinks, chocolate, tea etc) and other stimulants (including alcohol and sugary foods) at least throughout the evening

- Don't eat a heavy meal too close to bedtime because the effort required to digest it will reduce the quality of your sleep

- But also beware of going to bed hungry – some people find a warm drink e.g. milk particularly soothing

- Make your bedroom a place to sleep – if you study, watch TV or play video games there, take a break before getting ready for bed to allow your brain chance to unwind

- If pain keeps you awake, find natural remedies (e.g. to reduce inflammation) wherever possible to support your body's attempts to heal and make sure your mattress, pillows etc are not making the problems worse

- If you find your brain is buzzing with ideas, make a list of everything and keep a pad and pencil beside the bed in case you wake. This gives your brain permission to switch off rather than worrying about forgetting something

- Make sure your body is warm (bed socks and a hot water bottle may not be exciting but are essential if your feet are like icebergs); but that your room is cool, quiet and as dark as possible (even the light from your alarm clock can trick your body into thinking it is time to wake). For the same reason, if you need to get up in the night for the loo, try to avoid putting the main light on

- Establish a routine at night that encourages you to wind down: e.g. a bath is more relaxing than a shower; read a magazine or listen to soothing music. Go to bed and wake at the same time

- Sleep aids include earplugs, lavender essential oil (a few drops sprinkled on your pillow or nightwear), visualisation and other relaxation exercises

- If you find yourself getting agitated because you are unable to sleep, try counting your breaths and consciously slowing them down (e.g. feet breathing)

- Since emotional upset in particular can result in disturbed / unrefreshing sleep, nightmares etc seek counselling to identify and redress any unresolved issues rather than relying on prescription medication

Guidelines for Implementing a self-help programme

- apply the concept of **SMART** goals ie **S**pecific, **M**easurable, **A**chievable, **R**ealistic, **T**imed for short, medium and long-term changes (this is a reminder to break tasks into small but effective steps)
- read through the above and note any tips that you regularly include in your lifestyle (this helps build on positives) and any that can easily be incorporated to enhance well-being.
- avoid unrealistic goals, particularly those that involve a sense of being "deprived" of favourites or "pressured" against your natural inclination
- consider arranging for a mentor / coach to act as a sounding board and increase the likelihood of your staying on track

i. Getting going

1. Start to incorporate changes geared to:
   a) reducing adrenal overload
   b) ensuring effective elimination of toxins (bowels open at least daily)
   c) prioritising your own emotional needs – only by satisfying these will you be able to care for others

2. Work out a programme of rest, meditation, prayer etc **free from interruption.** Half an hour per day will allow you to recharge yourself and restore your ability to work productively - 'if you never say "no" what is your "yes" worth?'

ii. Anticipating pitfalls

1. Make a realistic assessment of your current functioning / energy levels during the next month / menstrual cycle (0 = bedbound – 10 = naturally energised). This means that future tasks can be scheduled for the most productive times and energy is not wasted on feeling guilty for having to postpone / cancel commitments

2. Note the specific "yes buts" that stop you applying the 70-30 rule (where you stop an activity whilst there is still 30% energy remaining, crucial if you are to replenish the energy overdraft that has accumulated)

3. Learn to recognise when and to what degree you

> - over-ride the body's "warning" signs re hunger, tiredness etc

> - rely on stimulants to provide energy and / or improve mood

> - feel guilty or frustrated at your perceived shortcomings

iii. Keeping going: Constantly evaluate progress – don't let setbacks or mistakes be anything other than a learning opportunity, but also be prepared to revise your goals accordingly

iv. **CELEBRATE successes!**

Printed in Great Britain
by Amazon

12211377R00153